Women of Achievement

Clara Barton

Women of Achievement

Abigail Adams

Susan B. Anthony

Tyra Banks

Clara Barton

Hillary Rodham Clinton

Marie Curie

Ellen DeGeneres

Diana, Princess of Wales

Helen Keller

Sandra Day O'Connor

Georgia O'Keeffe

Nancy Pelosi

Rachael Ray

Eleanor Roosevelt

Martha Stewart

Venus and Serena Williams

Women of Achievement

Clara Barton

HUMANITARIAN

Samuel Willard Crompton

CHELSEA HOUSE
PUBLISHERS

An imprint of Infobase Publishing

CLARA BARTON

Chelsea House
An imprint of Infobase Publishing
132 West 31st Street
New York, NY 10001

Library of Congress Cataloging-in-Publication Data
Crompton, Samuel Willard.
  Clara Barton : Humanitarian / by Samuel Willard Crompton.
      p. cm. — (Women of achievement)
  Includes bibliographical references and index.
  ISBN 978-1-60413-492-6 (hardcover)
  1. Barton, Clara, 1821-1912—Juvenile literature. 2. American Red Cross—Biography—Juvenile literature. 3. Nurses—United States—Biography—Juvenile literature. I. Title. II. Series.

  HV569.B3C76 2009
  361.7'634092—dc22
  [B]

                      2008055372

Chelsea House books are available at special discounts when purchased in bulk quantities for businesses, associations, institutions, or sales promotions. Please call our Special Sales Department in New York at (212) 967-8800 or (800) 322-8755.

You can find Chelsea House on the World Wide Web at http://www.chelseahouse.com

Series design by Erik Lindstrom
Cover design by Ben Peterson and Alicia Post

Printed in the United States of America

Bang EJB 10 9 8 7 6 5 4 3 2 1

This book is printed on acid-free paper.

All links and Web addresses were checked and verified to be correct at the time of publication. Because of the dynamic nature of the Web, some addresses and links may have changed since publication and may no longer be valid.

CONTENTS

The Blood of Antietam

Wednesday, September 17, 1862, was the seventy-fifth anniversary of the signing of the U.S. Constitution, a document that had been created through a series of compromises between North and South. That day was also destined to become the bloodiest day in U.S. history, as Union and Confederate forces clashed at Antietam, Maryland, in the first major battle of the Civil War to take place on Northern soil.

THE LONG RIDE

Four days earlier, Clara Barton had learned there would be a battle between Northern and Southern troops at Harpers Ferry. She went to the quartermaster-general in Washington, D.C., where she had lived for a number of years. Barton asked for a wagon in which to bring medical supplies to the front. The quartermaster-general agreed. The next day, Sunday, September 14, she received her means of transport: "I watched the approach of the long and high, white-covered, tortoise-motioned vehicle, with its string of little, frisky, long-eared animals, with the broad-shouldered driver astride, and the eternal jerk of the single rein by which he navigated his craft up to my door."[1] Clara Barton took no travel trunk that morning, only a few personal belongings tied up in her handkerchief. Then it was off to the front.

Barton and Reverend Cornelius Welles, who had become her tireless helper, arrived in the Harpers Ferry area too late to assist with anything. The tide of battle had moved on. Robert E. Lee, Stonewall Jackson, and the Army of Northern Virginia had won the battle at Harpers Ferry, and had then broken into separate groups. Now they were trying to reassemble at a place called Sharpsburg, on the northern side of the Potomac River.

George B. McClellan, commander of the Army of the Potomac, found himself in possession of the enemy's battle orders. A Confederate messenger had carelessly lost the papers, which told McClellan precisely where the Confederates were to be found. This was a golden opportunity for the Northern cause, the possibility to meet and destroy the Army of Northern Virginia while it was in pieces. But McClellan delayed his move, as he often did, and the Confederates had just enough time to gather 40,000 men at the village of Sharpsburg by the evening of September 16, 1862.

The night before, Clara Barton had taken a major risk. She and her wagon of precious medical supplies were at the very end of the long baggage train of the Union Army. She believed she was 10 miles (16 kilometers) away from the front of the army's procession. Barton, Reverend Welles, and a handful of others who had joined them would never get to the front in time to assist the wounded. Barton realized this, so at one in the morning on September 17, Barton reined up the horses and sped past dozens, if not hundreds of wagons that had pulled aside for the night. A few hours later, she was close to the front of the Union lines. When the Battle of Antietam began on the morning of September 17, Barton and her partners were in a position to help.

MORNING GUNS

General Joseph ("Fighting Joe") Hooker and his men led the first Union advance at about six in the morning. They advanced through a cornfield, only to be met with murderous musket and rifle fire from the Confederates. The Army of the Potomac had almost 80,000 men at the ready, but General McClellan sent only about half of them forward that morning. McClellan—a cautious, even timid general—had a habit of thinking his enemy had more men than was the case.

The Army of Northern Virginia fought on the defensive against the attacking North. The Southern men were superb shots, whether with the hunting rifle or the army musket. So, by the time Clara Barton and her group reached the Poffenberger Farm, there were already 300 men there. They lay on stretchers, awaiting assistance. She later recalled:

> Arriving at a little wicker gate, I found the dooryard of a small house, and myself face to face with one of the kindest and noblest surgeons I have ever met, Dr. Dunn, of Conneautville, Pennsylvania. Speechless both, for an instant, he at length threw up his hands with "God has indeed remembered us! How did you get from Virginia so soon? And again to supply our necessities![2]

An illustration of Union troops battling their way across Burnside Bridge at the Battle of Antietam during the American Civil War. Clara Barton gained her reputation as an extraordinary nurse during this battle.

Barton and Dr. Dunn had worked together after the Battle of Cedar Mountain a month earlier. But their joyful greeting was soon made serious by the needs of the moment. Dunn and a handful of other surgeons were running low on supplies for surgery. They had almost no bandages or rags, and they had already torn up every sheet they could find in the house. Luckily for them, Barton had brought many of the things they needed. Soon, the handful of surgeons were at work, with Barton and Reverend Welles assisting.

A SAVAGE AFTERNOON

During the Battle of Antietam, relatives and friends turned against each other to fight for their beliefs. There are legends of two brothers, each from a different side, meeting on the battlefield to fight. There is no record of this actually happening, but it is known that there were cousins and one-time neighbors drawn from communities along the Potomac River (the boundary between North and South) who fought each other with rifle, cannon, and bayonet. The fighting turned ugly by early afternoon, and the savagery increased with each charge. The Northern forces had the advantage and should have been able to smash the South, but the Army of Northern Virginia fought stubbornly throughout the afternoon. "Sunken" or "Bloody" Lane was named for the intensity of the fighting in that zone.

Meanwhile, Barton and her helpers were hard at work. Barton passed along the lines of stretchers and lines of men lying on the ground. To some she offered water; to others she brought a cool and steady hand. But in one case, she nearly came to her own end: "A man lying upon the ground asked for a drink. I stopped to give it, and having raised him

IN HER OWN WORDS

Although a trailblazing woman herself, Clara Barton was often oblivious to other women. According to William E. Barton, author of *The Life of Clara Barton, Founder of the American Red Cross*, Barton wrote in the hours before the Battle of Antietam: "In all this vast assemblage I saw no other trace of womankind." Yet there were quite a few women there, serving as laundresses and U.S. Army nurses!

with my right hand, was holding him. Just at this moment a bullet sped its free and easy way between us, tearing a hole in my sleeve and found its way into his body."[3] Barton chose never to mend that hole in her sleeve. Instead she kept it as a memento of the awfulness of war.

Another young man had a bullet inside his cheek. He asked Barton why it stung so much, and she replied that the bullet had not yet cooled. Turning white, he begged her to remove the bullet. Barton had never performed surgery before, but his desperation caused her to take action. Pulling a penknife from her pocket, she yanked out the bullet and then washed and bandaged his face. "I do not think a surgeon would have pronounced it a scientific operation," she wrote, "but that it was successful I dared to hope from the gratitude of the patient."[4]

By nightfall, Clara Barton's team of medical assistants had swelled to 30, but the number of wounded was in the thousands. This was a time of bleak despair for the surgeons, for they could not operate without light. Luckily, Barton had packed her wagon with a number of lanterns, which were soon hung, and the team continued its heroic work of saving those who could be saved.

TERRIBLE DAWN

Even Clara Barton, with her gift for narrative description, could not truly express how horrific the Battle of Antietam had been to those who participated in it. When September 18 dawned, about 11,000 Confederate soldiers and about 13,000 Union soldiers had been killed, wounded, or were missing. It was the costliest single-day battle in U.S. history. Barton did not know it yet, and would not know for months, but her little hometown of Oxford, Massachusetts, had sent a number of men to the battle, of whom about 20 were killed and wounded on that day.

Barton stayed for another 24 hours before returning home. Days later, she arrived in Washington, D.C., utterly exhausted. She fell into her sister's arms and went into a deep sleep. Her experiences had been some of the most nerve-wracking of anyone at the battle.

All the sacrifices had, to some extent, been in vain. George B. McClellan had won a victory but at a terrible cost, and he did not pursue Robert E. Lee and the Army of Northern Virginia. The war might have ended with a great victory for the Union at Antietam. Instead, the war would continue for another two and a half years.

Clara Barton made no comment on General McClellan's lost opportunity. She spent some weeks recovering from typhoid fever, which she had caught working at the battles of Stone Mountain and Antietam. Her efforts there won praise, most notably from Dr. Dunn. Writing to his wife, the doctor said: "Now what do you think of Miss Barton? In my feeble estimation, General McClellan, with all his laurels, pales beside the true heroine of the age, *the angel of the battlefield.*"[5]

Nothing But Fear

Years after her service to the wounded at the Battle of Antietam, Clara Barton, rich in age and in honors, looked back on her life. Many people thought she had nothing but courage in her veins, she said, for she had done one dangerous thing after another. When she thought of her childhood, however, she recalled, "I remember nothing but fear."

FAMILY

Clarissa Harlowe Barton was born on Christmas Day 1821, the third daughter and fifth child of Stephen Barton and Sarah Stone. Clarissa was named for a great-aunt who was about 50 years older than she. The aunt had been named for the heroine of Samuel Richardson's *Clarissa*, a novel that was much read at the time.

Clarissa is such a formal name that the Bartons began to call their youngest daughter "Clara," and this is how she signed her name throughout life. She was also known as "Baby," because her siblings—Dorothea, Stephen Jr., David, and Sally—were so much older. Sally was the closest to Barton in age, but even she was a decade older. Barton later recalled:

> I became the seventh member of a household con-
> sisting of the father and mother, two sisters and
> two brothers. . . . each one manifested an increasing
> personal interest in the newcomer, and as soon as
> developments permitted, set about instructing her in
> the various directions most in accord with the tastes
> and pursuits of each.[1]

In other words, Barton really had six parents: her father and mother, and her four elder siblings. There was much to learn from them.

Captain Stephen Barton was a bit younger than 50 when his last child was born. He had come of age in the 1790s and went west with the new U.S. Army to fight Indian tribes in what are now Ohio and Indiana (at the time called the Old Northwest). Upon his return from these battles, he was given a promotion and elected captain of his local militia group. He proudly wore that title throughout his life. He was a tall man who loved storytelling and moral instruction, and from the beginning he was Clara Barton's favorite. He was also the favorite of many of his neighbors, who thought him among the best of men—helpful, kind, and encouraging.

Sarah Stone Barton was as different from her warm husband as one might imagine. Strong, stout, and with a fearsome, powerful face, she was the member of the family who carried out the discipline. Where Stephen Barton could do no wrong, so far as his youngest daughter was concerned,

Sarah could do no right. Neighbors and friends tended to agree with Clara. They feared Mrs. Barton as much as they loved Captain Barton.

In Clara Barton's *The Story of My Childhood*, written when she was in her eighties, she describes how her father was one of the first horse breeders in the area. He and his son David became keen riders. David also became Clara's horseback riding teacher. He put her on one of the horses at the age of five and led her so well that she later wrote that sitting on horseback was as natural to her as reclining in an easy chair.

Her other brother, Stephen Jr., was her mentor in arithmetic and spelling. With the additional instruction provided by her two elder sisters (both of whom taught for a time) it was little wonder that Clara learned to read at a very early age. She delighted in most forms of learning and was proudest when she could demonstrate to her soldier father that she knew the difference between a major and a colonel, and between a sheet, line, and anchor.

Although she doubtlessly spent a great deal of time with her mother, Barton seldom mentions her in her autobiography and never suggests that she was a mentor. It seems as if the maternal affections came mostly from Clara's two elder

IN HER OWN WORDS

Clara Barton grew to love horses through her brother David and remained an equestrian throughout her life. According to William E. Barton, in his book *The Life of Clara Barton, Founder of the American Red Cross*, she later compared David to one of the most colorful horseman of the Old West: "He was the Buffalo Bill of the surrounding country."

sisters. It also seems that she was drawn more to "male" interests in her youth, rather than "female" ones. In one of the few comments Barton does make about her mother in *The Story of My Childhood*, she recalls:

> [My mother seemed] to conclude that there were plenty of instructors without her, attempted very little, but rather regarded the whole thing as a sort of mental conglomeration, and looked on with a kind of amused curiosity to see what they would make of it. Indeed, I heard her remark many years after, that I came out with a more level head than she would have thought possible.[2]

NEIGHBORHOOD

Clara Barton's hometown of North Oxford, Massachusetts, was an agricultural community on the verge of becoming a mill town. She had many relatives in the region, for the Bartons had been among the first settlers of Oxford, and there was every reason for young Clara to feel at ease in her surroundings. Even so, almost from the very beginning she had a sensitive, somewhat dark disposition. The sight of an ox being butchered when she was nine made her into a committed vegetarian. Thunderstorms could turn her miserable. She seemed, in general, too sensitive to be a Yankee farm girl. The same could be said about her elder sister Dorothea, who had a complete nervous breakdown around 1825 and spent the next 20 years as an invalid at the Barton home. Later in life, Barton did her best to disguise this fact, saying little of her sister; however, Dorothea's mental collapse likely had a major impact on Barton's life.

Barton's two brothers, Stephen Jr. and David, were handsome, wholesome young men, without any sign of the nervous disposition that distressed the girls. Still, they too had problems. Stephen and David went into partnership

The Clara Barton Birthplace Museum in North Oxford, Massachusetts, as photographed on July 15, 2002. The 11-room farmhouse is filled with memorabilia from Barton's remarkable life.

in the 1830s and started their own mill. They prospered for a time, but quite a few of their neighbors complained that the merchant sons of Captain Barton were not the same generous men as their father. Clara knew little of her neighbors' feelings about her brothers, who still were great heroes to her.

Young Clara had her first opportunity to demonstrate a talent for nursing when her brother David took ill in 1833. He had fallen from a rafter during the raising of a barn, and though he had gotten right back on his feet, he soon fell into what doctors called a delirious fever. It went on for almost two years. During those 24 months, Barton sat by his bed for hours at a time as his chief nurse. She applied live leeches to his skin to draw out "bad blood" (a common medical practice at the time) and prayed for his recovery.

MASSACHUSETTS IN THE 1830s AND 1840s

Clara Barton grew up at a time when her home state was going through significant changes. The generation that had fought in the Revolutionary War was dead and gone, and even men like Captain Barton, now in their sixties, were fading from the scene. The next generation had a different outlook on life.

At the time of Clara Barton's birth in 1821, most of Massachusetts looked as it had 50 or 100 years earlier. There were more people to be sure, but they still farmed, churned butter, and raised livestock as their parents and grandparents had done before them. In the 1830s, however, Massachusetts started to become a state of "mill towns," places where young men (and sometimes young women) earned their living by threading cotton or silk in the new factories. The lives of Captain Barton and his two sons provide a strong example of this change: Captain Barton's life was devoted to the farm, while his sons were industrialists.

Towns like Worcester—which the English novelist Charles Dickens had applauded as a neat, tidy place—became noted for chimneys, smokestacks, and grimy living conditions. Bigger towns and cities, such as New Bedford and Springfield, built paper mills. Other towns, such as Fitchburg and Leominster, specialized in the making of chairs, while Westfield eventually became known as "Whip City," because it made whips for the owners of buggies.

Critics of the change (and there were plenty) said it was turning Massachusetts from a farmer's paradise into a grimy, industrial, sweatshop world. Clara Barton, however, was never sentimental about the farming days of her youth. Though she loved horses, the farm had been a hard life, and she rejoiced in the many changes that took place throughout her long life. She lived long enough to see the electric light replace the kerosene lamp and for the automobile to begin to replace the horse and buggy.

Eventually, a new doctor in town told the Bartons to stop using the leeches, and David made a full recovery. The long ordeal not only demonstrated to the family how fragile life was, but also Clara's gifts as a nurse.

THE PHRENOLOGIST

Phrenology is the study of a person's character by tracing bumps on his or her head. The practice became common during Clara Barton's youth. One could say that it was a predecessor to psychology, in that practitioners of phrenology, called phrenologists, sought to understand their clients and to make recommendations for future conduct.

When Clara Barton was about 15 or 16, the noted phrenologist F.N. Fowler stopped by North Oxford. He spent a few days at the Barton homestead, where an anxious Sarah Barton asked him about her youngest child. Ever since Clara had stopped nursing David back to health, she had been back in a state of bashful shyness. At that time in New England, many people thought a person needed to be direct and assertive in life. Mrs. Barton appealed to the phrenologist to study Clara.

Fowler came up with an interesting and surprisingly accurate diagnosis. Admitting that Clara had a nervous temperament, he still urged the Bartons not to let that distress them. He said she would have to live with her temperament for the rest of her life, but he saw hope in Clara's restless spirit. "She will never assert herself for herself—she will suffer wrong first—but for others she will be perfectly fearless," Fowler predicted. "Throw responsibility upon her. She has all the qualities of a teacher. As soon as her age will permit, give her a school to teach."[3]

HER FIRST JOBS

Clara Barton was not pleased to hear that she was destined to be a teacher. Shy by nature, she disliked the idea of being placed before a school of pupils. Her first attempt at an occupation was working in her brothers' mill, but this ended when the mill burned down. Soon there was no choice but to venture into teaching. During this period, women had few other employment options. Both of her sisters, Dorothea and Sally, had also taught for a time. According to the traditions of New England, Yankee teenagers had to be useful—so now it was the youngest Barton child's turn.

Barton entered a schoolhouse as a teacher for the first time in 1839, at the age of 18. Some of her 40 pupils were almost the same age. And at just 5 feet tall (1.5 meters), Barton hardly had the kind of physical presence that commanded respect from the unruly members of her class. The phrenologist proved correct: Barton could assert herself much better when she spoke of the rights and needs of others, not of herself.

When a handful of boys acted out, Barton tried to reason with them. When they scorned her as a weak female, she ran and played with them at recess, which demonstrated her spirit. But when one of the boys became exceptionally difficult and resisted her authority, she used a whip on him. The female students gasped! The boys were astounded. The misbehaving boy fell to the floor after receiving several blows.

That was it for corporal punishment. Barton kept her whip by her, school year after school year, but she never had to use it again. Instead, she won over her students through a combination of friendliness and leadership. If she felt unqualified to teach, it was because she believed that she did not know enough, either of her subject matter or of the philosophy of education. Despite these feelings, she was a success in the Oxford schools, winning awards for having the best-disciplined school year after year.

Barton's parents were pleased with her success as a teacher and they doubtlessly hoped she would soon find a

Clara Barton, as seen in a portrait painted by Henry Inman in 1844.

man to marry. Though she was a solid and capable woman, there were few courtships in Barton's early life. Many historians have been keen to find an answer as to why this was so. It is possible that one reason was Barton's physical plainness—her face was round and her ruddy cheeks were too prominent for the beauty standards of the time.

There were few suitors during her teen years, and even fewer during the decade she taught in Oxford. Perhaps this was because she devoted herself to her job, but it is also possible that she turned off young men with her own masculinity. Barton never looked like a man, and she never dressed like one, but her early closeness with her father had a great impact on her. Even while performing a "womanly" occupation such as teaching, she did it in a way that sometimes demonstrated "manly" characteristics.

In her letters and diaries, Barton seldom mentions suitors during her teaching years. As she grew older she seems to have accepted the idea that she would remain single. Very few people of that time chose to remain unmarried, but it was by no means embarrassing to be single. Many people, particularly women, found a place of dignity either in the home of relatives or in some kind of occupation.

Years passed and Barton grew older. By the time she turned 29, she was hungry to leave her hometown and state. She had little experience of the outside world, but she wished to see some of it. In 1851, she applied and was accepted to the Clinton Liberal Institute in upstate New York, one of the few colleges that accepted female students.

As she prepared to leave for school, the little world in which Barton had grown up was already fading. Her father's health remained strong, but he was no longer a leader of the town as he once had been. Her mother's health was not good, and Barton had little comfort to offer the woman who seems to have left her to be raised by her siblings. Her sister Dorothea had died a few years before. Her brothers were healthy and hearty, but there were conflicts and difficulties in their business affairs.

Barton's brothers took her to the Worcester train station the morning she left. The child whom they had once called "Baby" and "Tot" was leaving for a bigger life.

A Man's World

Clara Barton was not a feminist in the modern meaning of the word. She believed that men and women were meant to do different things in life, but she wished greater freedom in her own life. She found this freedom when she left home.

Barton had long felt that her own education was not enough, that she needed more to offer to her pupils. It made sense, therefore, for her to continue her studies at the Clinton Liberal Institute, which was located in the same town as Hamilton College.

Since Barton was a small woman, it was easy for her to pass herself off as just another young person beginning her education. Whether from modesty or a desire to avoid unnecessary attention, she did not tell her fellow students that she had already taught for the better part of a decade. As a result, they saw her as one of their fellows.

As a student, Barton took every course on the schedule and tried to fit in independent-study courses as well. Her hunger for education would continue for the rest of her life. Barton felt she had been brought up in a kind of bubble and almost always looked for ways to expand her knowledge.

Barton also made several new friends in Clinton, but the most lasting was with the school principal, Louisa Barker, who saw something special in the woman from Massachusetts. There was also a new friendship with Mary Norton from New Jersey, and a flirtation with Mary's brother Charles. There were horseback rides in the country and picnics that raised Barton's spirits so she seldom felt gloomy. At Clinton, she began to feel stronger about herself as an individual and increasingly separate from her family in Oxford.

FAMILY TROUBLE

During this time of learning and discovery, Barton also faced hardships within her family. In May 1851, Barton learned that her beloved brother Stephen had been charged with bank robbery in nearby Otsego County, New York. Although he was found not guilty, the charge alone was enough to persuade most of his Massachusetts customers to cut their connections with his business. Soon, Stephen was financially on the rocks.

Around the same time, Barton learned that her mother had died at home in Oxford. Although they had never been close, the news was still shocking. Her father moved in with her sister Sally and her family. Sarah Barton's death, combined with Stephen's trouble with the law, further cut Clara Barton's ties with central Massachusetts.

When Barton graduated from Clinton in the spring of 1851, the occasion was not as joyous as she might have hoped. Though she had excelled in her academic work, there seemed no other future for her apart from teaching, and, for the moment, she wished to avoid returning to her Massachusetts hometown. She wished to see more of the world and to discover what her place in it would be.

Barton spent two months with friends before returning to Oxford, where she felt more out of place than ever. Her sister Sally—whose husband had turned out to be a poor provider—was happy with her two children, but the Barton family as a whole lived under the shadow of Stephen Jr.'s trouble with the law. Her father was growing frail. Clara Barton spent some months at home, penning diary entries that suggest a severe depression, before she accepted an invitation to Bordentown, New Jersey, to live for a period with the Nortons, whom she had come to know at Clinton, New York.

A NEW SCHOOL

Barton found life with the Nortons rather overwhelming. A large, bustling family, its members had little sense of the kind of space and privacy to which Barton was accustomed. She constantly felt pressed to dress up, to go out, and to be sociable in all sorts of ways. She coped rather well at first but then decided she needed to work. In October 1851, she began teaching at what is said to have been the first public school in New Jersey.

Barton was used to the Massachusetts school system, where elementary education had recently become mandatory. This was not the case with New Jersey, and she found herself having to propose, and then defend, the idea of mandatory education. There was also a belief, common in New Jersey and elsewhere during this period, that teachers should be paid directly from the tuition of the children.

A recent photo of the Clara Barton Schoolhouse in Bordentown, New Jersey. The school, founded by Barton, was one of the first free public schools in New Jersey.

This often meant that if the school had very few students, educators would have to work without much pay at all.

Months later, Barton started a public school of her own in Bordentown, New Jersey, located about 10 miles (16 km) away from the Nortons' home. Barton entered the project with all her usual energy. She encountered tough farm boys, much like those back in Oxford, but they proved no match for her skillful combination of affection, learning, and discipline. The school was soon a huge success, and the people of Bordentown approved a large amount of funding to ensure the school would continue to operate.

Unfortunately, Barton was crushed to learn that she, the founder, had been cast aside as the new principal. The job would instead go to a man.

In the spring of 1854, she resigned her teaching position. Although her main reason for leaving was heartache over having been displaced by a man, she had also developed what seemed like an allergic reaction to the building itself. The allergies had caused her to lose her voice. For the rest of her long life, Barton would typically lose her voice when under stress.

THE CAPITAL CITY

Barton could have returned to Oxford, but each passing year made her less willing to return to her hometown. Instead, in the summer of 1854, she went to Washington, D.C. Although it was the nation's capital, Washington was not the large city it is today. Back then it had only about 10,000 inhabitants, and many of them were family members of senators and representatives who considered the districts they represented to be their true homes.

The year Barton arrived, 1854, was the year the Kansas-Nebraska Act was proposed in Congress. Years had passed since the last great crisis between North and South; the introduction of this bill brought on another. The question was whether the newly organized territories of Kansas and Nebraska would be open to slavery. Senator Stephen Douglas of Illinois argued for "popular sovereignty," meaning that the people of those regions should decide. But that had the potential to overturn the Missouri Compromise of 1820, which prohibited slavery north of latitude 36°30' except within the boundaries of the state of Missouri.

Barton's letters and diaries from this period show that she was little concerned with the problems between the North and South. She wanted work, *needed* work, and she found it in the U.S. Patent Office.

TIES AND CONTACTS

Barton came to Washington without influence or people to assist her, but she soon found a small group of men who became useful to her. One was Alexander DeWitt, the congressman from her district in Massachusetts, and the other was Charles Mason, the commissioner of patents. The U.S. Patent Office was in its infancy when Barton arrived in Washington, but the latter half of the nineteenth century would see boom times for the organization. Upon meeting Barton, Commissioner Mason was so impressed with her that he asked her to be governess to his daughter. When a vacancy opened in the clerk section of the Patent Office, Mason recommended her appointment.

In July 1854, when Barton entered the Patent Office, it employed about 20 clerks. The clerks painstakingly copied patent applications by hand and made sure that they complied with federal guidelines. Barton earned $1,400 in her first year, partly because of her efficiency and fine handwriting. Her salary was an excellent one for a woman in the 1850s, and Barton was able, for the first time in her life, to save some of the money she earned. For a time, she thought she might spend her entire working life at the Patent Office, slowly putting away enough money to enjoy a respectable retirement. But, as so often in her life, other matters changed her plans.

THE NEW ADMINISTRATION

In 1856, James Buchanan, a Democrat from Pennsylvania, was elected president. He came into office on March 4, 1857, and Barton found herself out of work. Many people knew of her sympathies for the Republican Party, and that was enough for her to be removed from the government payroll. Barton, who had enjoyed more security and pleasure in her three years at the Patent Office than in any earlier part of her life, was again out of work.

She returned to Oxford and lived with her brother David and his wife, Julie. Once there, Barton found that the sleepy community had changed greatly in the last decade. Her beloved brother Stephen had just pulled up stakes and moved to eastern North Carolina, where he believed he would find steadier (and cheaper) labor. Her beloved father was still Captain Barton to one and all, a grand old man,

NORTH AND SOUTH IN THE 1850s

As a Northerner, Clara Barton did not often think about slavery. Her upbringing in rural Massachusetts was so far removed from the institution that she did not meet black people—whether slave or free—until her late teens. The farming communities and mill towns of the North were so different from the plantation society of the South that she could scarcely imagine what the South was like.

By the time Barton first moved to Washington, D.C., there had already been several great crises between North and South, each one followed by a great compromise. The question of whether to admit Missouri to the Union, brought up in 1819, had resulted in the Compromise of 1820. Under this compromise, Missouri came in as a slave state and Maine (sectioned off from Massachusetts) came in as a free state. Then there was the Nullification Crisis of 1832, brought on by a high tariff that harmed Southern farmers. This crisis was resolved when South Carolina backed down from its insistence to the right of "nullification" (a legal theory that suggests a state has the right to invalidate any federal law which it deems unconstitutional) and when the North agreed to but his strength was weakened. Barton's sister Sally, who had spent the past decade raising her two children without much help from her husband, needed Barton's help.

Barton intended her return to be a short one, but it lasted for about two years. In that time, she had almost no well-paid employment, but her habit of saving kept her financially secure. Her much more pressing concern was

lower the tariff. The Crisis of 1850 had been resolved by the Compromise of 1850, under which California came in as a free state. The South, for its part, received a much tougher fugitive slave law, requiring Northern sheriffs to assist Southerners who went north looking for runaway slaves.

By choosing to live in Washington, Barton suddenly became much more aware of the tug-of-war between North and South. Politically, she favored the brand-new Republican Party, who nominated John C. Frémont for president in 1856. Frémont and the Republicans spoke of "free soil, free labor, and free men." This did not mean they were outright abolitionists, but that they resisted the expansion of slavery into any of the new territories that entered the Union.

Barton would later become a fierce defender of rights for African Americans and was much beloved by the black community. But in the 1850s, she was just another Northerner who did not truly understand the differences between North and South. The same could be said for many of the lawmakers who voted for the Kansas-Nebraska Act of 1854. The two sections, North and South, would know little peace from that time forward.

that she had so much free time, which weighed on her spirit far more than an abundance of tasks. Her most useful occupation in 1857 and 1858 was looking after her beloved nephew, Sally's son, who had come down with tuberculosis. Despite a visit to Minnesota for what was called the "prairie cure," he continued to weaken. There was also a niece, who frequently asked Barton for money.

It was with considerable relief that Barton learned that the U.S. Patent Office would again hire her, though as a temporary clerk with a reduced rate of pay. Returning to Washington, Barton found a less pleasant work environment than she had known in the past. The best the Patent Office could give her was pay by the copied word, which, if she worked like a demon, came out to about $900 per year. Though it was a significant pay cut from her previous government work, Barton went right back to her former task.

SECESSION AND WAR

Republican Abraham Lincoln of Illinois was elected president in November 1860 and inaugurated in March 1861. During the time between Lincoln's election and inauguration, the country slid toward civil war. In his last four months of office, President James Buchanan did little to prevent South Carolina and six other Southern states from adopting ordinances of secession, meaning that they left the Union. President-elect Lincoln was known for his strong pro-Union stance, but he gave little hint as to what policy he would adopt to deal with the Southern secession crisis.

In the four months between the election and the inauguration, Barton worked steadily in Washington, D.C. She was pleased to be back at her old work but she was worried, and sometimes appalled, at what was happening in the country. Like many Northerners, Barton did not believe in the Southern idea of secession from the Union, and she hoped the Southern states could be talked out of it. When pressed on the matter, she recalled the ideas and values of her soldier father: The Union *would* be preserved, come what may.

Barton went to Abraham Lincoln's inauguration on March 4, 1861, but a bad cold kept her from attending the inaugural ball. She thought well of Lincoln from the beginning, but like so many other people, Northerners and Southerners, she did not immediately appreciate the great qualities he hid beneath his homespun appearance.

Then, on April 12, came momentous news: The people of Charleston, South Carolina, had fired on Fort Sumter in Charleston Harbor. The War Between the States, today called the Civil War, had begun.

Follow the Cannon

Years later, when asked how she found the place where she was most needed, Clara Barton answered firmly, "Follow the cannon." Throughout the Civil War, she wanted to be where the action was thickest, which allowed her to be where her help was most needed.

BOYS IN BLUE

The Union forces at Fort Sumter surrendered after a 24-hour bombardment. President Lincoln then issued a call for 75,000 men to volunteer to fight to preserve the Union. Back in Oxford, Massachusetts, old Stephen Barton complained that the president had not called for 300,000 men.

Men turned out to volunteer in every town, village, and city of the North. Some enlisted out of a desire for adventure, while others felt a deeper purpose to hold the nation together. Others spoke of making a better future, one in which all men were truly free and equal.

Oxford and the surrounding community quickly created Company E of the 6th Massachusetts Regiment (which was later reformed into the 15th Massachusetts Regiment), and Barton learned with pride that many of her former pupils, now men of farming and business, had rushed to join. Her first opportunity to be of service came when the Massachusetts regiment passed through Baltimore, Maryland, on its way to Washington, D.C.

Baltimore was a divided city, with the local government and leading officials supporting the Union but much of the population in favor of the South. As the 6th Regiment got off of one set of train cars to transfer to another in Baltimore, a mob descended upon it, throwing rotten eggs and stones and firing the occasional gun. The soldiers held their fire most of the time, but they were under severe stress. When they did fire, a number of civilians were killed or wounded. So were about six men of the regiment.

When the Massachusetts regiment came to Washington, D.C., Barton was among those waiting at the train depot. She brought umbrellas, knapsacks, and all sorts of materials that the soldiers were lacking. It remains a puzzle how she had the foresight to bring these things while government officials had not. Barton found a number of her former pupils in the ranks. Trooping off to Washington, she sat among them, reading Massachusetts newspapers to keep them amused. "You would have smiled to see me and my audience in the Senate Chamber of the U.S.," she wrote home. "Oh! But it was better attention than I have been accustomed to see there in the old times."[1]

Barton immediately became a collector of clothing, supplies, and medicines, all of which were badly needed. She collected these items in and around Washington. She also organized a relief effort in her hometown of Oxford, asking local women to collect things for the Union soldiers. Like nearly everyone at the time, Barton did not realize how bloody and destructive the Civil War would be, but at least she had the foresight to take action.

Just as the Union soldiers, "the boys in blue," were gathering in Washington, "the boys in grey" (the Confederate soldiers of the Southern states) were forming in Richmond, Virginia. Barton and the rest of Washington waited anxiously for the first major battle of the war.

BLOODY DAYS

The First Battle of Bull Run, which the Confederates called the Battle of Manassas, took place on July 21, 1861. More than 30,000 brightly dressed Union soldiers clashed with an equal number of Confederates. When the day was over, the Union Army was in full retreat. Together from both sides, about 5,000 men had been killed, wounded, or left missing.

Barton was not present at Bull Run, but many Washington society ladies were there, brought along on carriages and with picnic lunches for the occasion. This kind of joyous, breezy optimism soon disappeared. Despite the hopes of many that the war would be a quick one, the Battle of Bull Run showed everyone that this would not be the case.

Up to this point, Barton had acted entirely alone in her aid to the soldiers. She had no rank or station with the Union Army, no pass given by any of the commanders. She was simply a Northern woman doing what she considered her duty. An opportunity to join an organization came with the creation of the U.S. Sanitary Commission in the autumn

BATTLE OF BULL RUN.

An illustration depicting the Battle of Bull Run on July 21, 1861, one of the most significant clashes of the Civil War.

of 1861. A group of New York businessmen created the commission, the first government effort to bring together the instruments of movement (horses and ambulances) with those of relief (bandages, medicine, and the like).

Barton, however, never applied to become a nurse in the Sanitary Commission. To do so would go against her independent spirit; she preferred to work with as few regulations as possible. During the second half of 1861, she continued to collect medicines and supplies, and waited for the moment when she would most be needed.

ONE LAST SUMMONS

In the winter of 1861 to 1862, Barton went home to tend to her father. Stephen Barton was 88 years old and in failing health. Barton did her best to encourage him, telling stories of the war that was then unfolding, but he did not respond as he had in the past. He stopped eating sometime in the winter but still hung on to life until March.

One of Barton's last conversations with her father revolved around what she might do for the war effort. One might think that her early shyness and uncertainty had deserted her, but this was not the case: She still wondered if she could do anything worthwhile. The old

DOROTHEA DIX

The chief of U.S. Army nurses during the Civil War had an upbringing somewhat like that of Clara Barton, but the two women's personalities could not have been more different. Born in Maine in 1802, Dorothea Dix was raised in part by her Boston grandparents. Her family was poor, and she had no choice but to enter the teaching profession at an early age. She showed talent in this profession, but then she contracted tuberculosis. After that happened, she became more interested in the lives of the mentally ill.

Dix visited her first jail in 1841, in Cambridge, Massachusetts. She was appalled by the conditions and by the fact that mentally ill people were thrown together with common criminals. Inspired to help, she began a lifetime crusade as an advocate for the mentally ill. She helped to establish hospitals for the mentally ill in a number of states. By the start of the Civil War, she was a famous international figure who enjoyed meetings with Queen Victoria and Pope Pius IX.

In June 1861, Dix became superintendent of all U.S. Army nurses, a post she held for the duration of the Civil War. She was captain's answer was that she must, as the daughter of a soldier and of a Mason, help wherever she could. (A Mason is a member of a secret fraternal organization that arose in Europe in the late sixteenth and early seventeenth centuries.) "As a patriot he bade me serve my country with all I had, even my life if need be," she wrote. "As the daughter of an accepted Mason, he bade me seek and comfort the afflicted everywhere, and as a Christian he

not as successful in her nursing efforts as she had been in the field of mental health. Dix was, if anything, too careful about sticking to rules and too concerned with social correctness. Her early advertisements made clear that only "plain looking" women over the age of 30 would be considered for the nursing profession, since she was worried that pretty, young nurses would gain a bad reputation for hanging around male soldiers all day.

Dix was unpopular with her staff and even with her trainees (she helped train about 180 young women, including the future novelist Louisa May Alcott). Despite her unpopularity, she nevertheless received recognition for her services from the secretary of war in 1866. After the war, Dix returned to her efforts on behalf of the mentally ill. She died in Trenton, New Jersey, in 1887.

Although Barton and Dix were different in temperament and personality, both women were greatly honored at their deaths, and both helped to forward the cause of those normally forgotten by society.

charged me to honor God and love mankind." One of Stephen Barton's last acts was to give his daughter his gold Masonic badge, which she kept for the rest of her life.[2] The old soldier died on March 21, 1862.

A NEW CAMPAIGN

Barton's father left her a small farm in Oxford. Along with the money she had saved from her government work, Barton was as close to economic independence as she had ever been. But this was a small part of her thoughts at the time. Her father was gone, her brother Stephen lived in North Carolina, and her nephew was ill with tuberculosis. As much as she might do for her family, it never seemed to be enough to win her a secure place in the community. She felt pushed to leave and seek the wider world, as she had done so often in the past.

Barton returned to Washington in April and spent much of that spring and summer organizing her growing stock of medical supplies. There were Ladies' Aid societies, some organized by her friends, which sent large quantities of food, clothing, and bandages to her. Barton needed a warehouse in which to place it all, but she did not have one. These supplies would be greatly needed as the Civil War entered a new, deadlier phase.

At about the same time Barton returned to the capital city, General George B. McClellan led the Army of the Potomac by water to southeast Virginia. The movement was intended to avoid a long march to their destination, Richmond, Virginia. But McClellan, who was a splendid organizer and creator of discipline, was not an imaginative or daring field commander. He consistently convinced himself that General Robert E. Lee and the Army of Northern Virginia had more men than he did. As it turned out, the reverse was true.

By July 1862, McClellan and his army were in a full, orderly retreat back to Washington. Meanwhile, the daring commanders of the Army of Northern Virginia, Robert E. Lee and Stonewall Jackson, were advancing rapidly toward Washington. The Confederates beat the Union forces at the Second Battle of Bull Run, and for a time seemed ready to take Washington. During this crisis, Barton was eager to get into the action and do something of value for the Union soldiers in the field. Years later, she recalled:

> When our armies fought on Cedar Mountain [Virginia], I broke the shackles and went to the field. Five days and nights with three hours' sleep—a narrow escape from capture—and some days of getting the wounded into hospitals at Washington brought Saturday, August 30. And if you chance to feel that the positions I occupied were rough and unseemly for a woman—I can only reply that they were rough and unseemly for men.[11]

In writing that she had broken "the shackles," Barton meant that she had finally received permission to travel to the front. For months, she had pleaded with army commanders to be allowed to minister to the men in the field, but it was a lucky encounter with Quartermaster Daniel Rucker that won her permission. There were horrendous casualties in the fighting, and neither the Sanitary Commission nor Dorothea Dix's nurses could do everything at once, so Colonel Rucker gave Barton a pass that enabled her to come and go as she pleased. He never intended for her to be on the battlefield itself. She simply took that liberty.

MISTAKEN IDENTITY

One of Barton's most memorable moments on the battlefield came soon after receiving Colonel Rucker's pass. With a wagonload of supplies, a driver, and Reverend Welles with her, she hurried to the battlefront. Upon arriving at the place where the wounded were held, Barton came upon an especially desperate case, a young man who mistook her for his sister, Mary: "The illusion was complete; the act had done the falsehood my lips refused to speak. I can never forget the cry of joy, 'Oh Mary! Mary! You have come? I knew you would come if I called you and I have called you for so long. I could not die without you, Mary.'"[4]

The young man's hot tears trickled down from his cheeks onto Barton's clothing. She held him all night long, and when morning came, she badgered the Union surgeon to take this young man to a hospital in Washington. Her demand was refused. "Oh, impossible, madam, he is mortally wounded and will never reach the hospital. We must take those who have a hope of life."[5] Barton pointed out that many of those being taken aboard the train had only a 50 percent chance of survival. What harm would it do for this young man to have a feeling of comfort in his last hours? The surgeon gave in.

Days later, on reaching the back of the Union lines, Barton learned what had happened to that soldier. He had died hours before, but the attending surgeon assured her that his mother and the real Mary had both reached him before the end.

That was enough for Barton. It had to be, for she had many more challenges ahead.

Gunpowder Blue

As was told in the opening chapter, Barton reached the battlefield of Antietam in time to be of great service to hundreds of wounded Union soldiers. It was the single bloodiest day of U.S. history. She remained at Antietam for two more days, before returning to Washington, utterly exhausted. When she looked in the mirror, she saw that her normally fair skin had turned a dull blue that came from exposure to gunpowder.

FREDERICKSBURG

By mid-autumn 1862, Barton had become a success in her own right. She had been a fine teacher and a competent and efficient copyist for the Patent Office, but nothing she had done in her life to that point equaled the satisfaction she felt from tending to wounded men on the battlefield. For the first time in her life, she began to move out of the edginess and insecurity that had haunted her from childhood.

Barton was also beginning to get patrons—men and women who believed in her cause of bringing relief to soldiers on the battlefield. One of her strongest allies was Senator Henry Wilson of Massachusetts. Having had a hardscrabble childhood in New Hampshire, Wilson admired those who made the best of a bad situation. Colonel Rucker had been the first to say "yes" to Barton's desire to be of service, but Senator Wilson was her second patron—and in many ways her most important one. Soon, others joined the chorus of those who admired Clara Barton's work.

How did Barton earn such support? There is no simple answer, for Barton was a complex person. She was so self-less in moments of danger, so giving of herself, that she seemed at times to be the definition of self-sacrifice. On a battlefield where thousands of men were trying to kill each other, Barton and others like her seemed to many to be sent

IN HER OWN WORDS

According to William E. Barton's *The Life of Clara Barton, Founder of the American Red Cross*, Clara Barton, in a letter to a cousin, described the help Senator Henry Wilson of Massachusetts was giving her, but also noted: "Oh yes, he *is* married." The expression indicates that she was aware of the fact that this was one of the many times in her life when she found an already married man to admire. Yet she did not regret never having married. In 1911, at the age of 90, she confided to her diary, "After all, *Aloneness* is not the worst thing in the world."

from heaven. Nowhere did her courage come to the surface more strongly than at the Battle of Fredericksburg, fought in December 1862.

After President Lincoln removed General McClellan as commander of the Army of the Potomac, the new commander, General Ambrose Burnside, led Union forces forward in December. With the army on its march south, Barton had some premonitions of what would follow when the Union soldiers came to a crossing place over the Rappahannock River.

The Union Army attacked on the morning of December 13, crossing a set of rickety bridges that had been set up for the attack. The Army of Northern Virginia was concealed within the town and dug in at Marye's Heights overlooking the scene. The Confederates poured cannon shot and rifle fire into the Union men, who struggled to cross the river and then fought to take the town. The entire affair was a disaster, with thousands of men falling. On Marye's Heights, General Lee is said to have commented, "It is well that war is so terrible, or we should grow too fond of it."[1]

Barton was on the north side of the Rappahannock River, tending the wounded coming in on stretchers. There were so many she could not count them, and she had no time to take a breath. The moments seemed like hours. Then came a handwritten message from a surgeon working on the south side of the river, "Come, your place is here."[2]

Gathering up her skirts, Barton ran across the same rickety bridges that had seen the deaths of so many Union soldiers. Gunfire splattered near her, so close it seemed certain she would die, but she continued. The wood on the last section of the bridge had nearly given way, and a gallant officer helped her to cross. She soon found the hospital where the surgeon was working. Just a half an hour later, the Union officer who had helped her across the bridge was brought before her, mortally wounded. Barton seemed fated

Fallen soldiers lie before the Dunker Church on the battlefield at Antietam during the Civil War.

to experience the battle—and the war—in a very personal way. Hours later she came upon another wounded man:

> I knelt by him and commenced with fear and trembling ... After some hours' labor, I began to recognize features. They seemed familiar. With what impatience I wrought. Finally my hand wiped away the last obstruction. An eye opened and there to my gaze was the sexton of my old home church![3]

No one knows how many men Barton tended during the Battle of Fredericksburg, but it is believed that over the next week she came into contact with almost every wounded man in each hospital that had been set up for the wounded. Although her name had become known after the Battle of Antietam, her service at the Battle of Fredericksburg brought her undying fame. For decades to come, veterans of the conflict would periodically visit her, each one claiming she had saved his life. As courageous as the Fredericksburg soldiers were, Barton's name came to stand out as the highest example of what could be accomplished in the heat of battle. However, she never tasted such heights of success again.

BROTHER DAVID

At the beginning of 1863, Barton learned that she would lose her friend and assistant, Reverend Welles, who needed to return to his church. Barton felt the loss deeply, since she knew it was necessary for her to have a man with her when she was needed on the battlefield. As it turned out, her brother David would be the next man to help her. Today, it is unclear whether she made it happen, or whether she allowed it to happen, but her older brother was made a quartermaster in the Union Army.

David did not wish to go to war. His wife felt the same way. He and his wife were already irritated with Barton for having persuaded their 15-year-old son to enlist in the Union Army. The last thing they needed was for David, now in his mid-fifties, to leave for the front. Yet, when the orders came through from Washington (Senator Henry Wilson had arranged them), David left Oxford to join the army—and his sister. In the spring of 1863, Barton and her brother sailed from New York City, bound for the Sea Islands of South Carolina.

ANOTHER WORLD, A DIFFERENT LIFE

Even today, the Sea Islands off the Atlantic Coast are very different from other parts of the country. There is a Caribbean feel to the islands, but there is also a profound sense of isolation from the mainland. This was even more the case in 1863, when Barton and her brother joined the Union forces there.

After Barton and her brother settled into quarters established for the quartermaster, she began to enjoy life on the Sea Islands. So far, her experience of the Civil War had been of the hardest sort, seeing the dead, helping the wounded, and witnessing the poor state of the medical services. But at Hilton Head, she encountered gentleman soldiers, some

OXFORD IN THE CIVIL WAR

When the Civil War began in 1861, Oxford, Massachusetts, seemed to be a town that time had forgotten. Indeed, Barton had often felt that way herself. Yet, like so many other small communities, Oxford turned out a major effort for the War Between the States.

Oxford replied to President Lincoln's first call for volunteers by forming what eventually became Company E of the 15th Massachusetts Regiment. Over the next four years, Company E produced a total of 19 officers, 82 privates, 41 recruits, and 20 draftees (all of whom were drafted in the summer of 1863). Oxford men fought in most of the major Civil War engagements, with some of their greatest losses coming at Antietam. In that battle, seven of the small town's men were killed, and many wounded.

of whom reminded her of her father. There was Colonel
Lamb, a Massachusetts man whose father had been a doctor to the Bartons in Oxford. There was also Colonel John
Elwell from Michigan. Tall, lean, and handsome with a thick
beard, Elwell was what many Union officers most wished to
be: gentlemanly, highly educated, and with a strong sense of
duty. In his company, Barton found the first true intellectual
companionship she had enjoyed for some time. They read
together, composed some poetry, and also enjoyed many
horseback rides along the edge of the Sea Islands. Barton was
in love, for perhaps the first time in her life.

Men had pursued Barton at different times over the
years, but she had rejected them for one reason or another.

Often, Barton ended up caring for men she had known
as boys. Today, when the U.S. population is more than 300
million, it seems incredible that Barton would meet so many
people she knew on the battlefield. It must be understood,
however, that the entire U.S. population during the Civil
War—white, black, male, female, North and South—came to
only about 30 million.

When the war ended, most of the Oxford men returned to
their hometown. A large number of them had been shoemakers
prior to the war, and many returned to that occupation. Very
likely, many of them would have said that the war had a great
impact on their lives. The Civil War was a great dividing point
for many people who lived in the 1860s, splitting their recollec-
tions of life's events into "before" and "after" the war.

Those who knew her best suspected it was because she never found a man who resembled the values and virtues of her soldier father. John Elwell had these qualities and more; his intellectual passion echoed her own. There was only one difficulty: He was married.

Barton's letters and diaries from this time suggest that she and Colonel Elwell had a passionate relationship, but she was always discrete enough not to say so outright. She and the colonel may have shared a strong intimacy, but it was always shadowed by the knowledge that he would one day return to his wife and children. Colonel Elwell's letters to Barton suggest that he returned her affections in full. This was, quite possibly, the happiest time in Barton's life.

The same could not be said for David Barton. This may, in fact, have been among the worst of times in his life. David was not suited to be a quartermaster, or anything else in the military. He was no longer the energetic, horseback-riding brother Barton remembered from youth. He was passing from middle age to old age. David resented the duties of quartermaster, and his son proved a poor soldier, running the first time a shot was fired in his direction.

Logically, Barton knew of her brother's lack of soldier skills, but family loyalty meant she did not pay attention to them. She continued to believe David would shake off his hesitation and prove himself worthy of the Barton name. At the same time, she and David were quite concerned about their eldest brother, Stephen. He had moved to North Carolina in the mid 1850s and was still there when the Civil War began. They had heard nothing from him in more than two years.

FORT WAGNER

In the early summer of 1863, Barton's time with Colonel Elwell was jarred when he was called to leave for the front. He, like Barton and most of the men stationed at Hilton Head, were assigned the difficult task of invading

Charleston, South Carolina, where the Civil War had begun two and a half years earlier. There was a great desire on the part of the Union to see Charleston surrender. Charleston's

FRANCES GAGE

The life story of Frances Dana Barker Gage was much like Barton's, with the notable exception that Gage had married and had nine children. Born in Ohio in 1808, Gage showed impatience with "women's roles" at an early age. She married an attorney at the age of 21, and they raised a large family, while moving from Ohio to St. Louis, Missouri, then back to Ohio again. In 1851 and 1853, Gage led Ohio state conventions on the rights of women. By the time she met Barton in 1863, Gage was a well-known feminist.

Gage had no official role in the Sea Islands; she was there simply because she wanted to be. She and Barton struck up a wonderful friendship, with Gage, who was 13 years older than Barton, acting as the leader and confidante. Barton took to calling her "Mother," and Gage became, in many ways, the feminine guiding influence that Barton had never had.

Barton and Gage wrote poetry together, which centered on the themes of war and dislocation, but with an emphasis on humor. They joked about themselves as "two old women" sitting around a campfire. In addition to deep friendship, Gage introduced Barton to new beliefs about liberty and equality. Barton had never been a strong abolitionist, until she met "Mother" Gage. Barton's belief in the rights of women had already been strong, but her time with Gage increased that, too. It is not too much to say that Gage was a key mentor for Barton, and that Barton came away from her Sea Island experience a more fully rounded person. The two friends stayed in contact for the rest of their lives.

harbor, however, was guarded by numerous island forts. The strongest of these was Fort Wagner on Morris Island.

It was at this time that Barton first became aware of African-American soldiers. Growing up, she had met almost no black people, and her years in Washington, D.C., had made her no more sympathetic than the average Northerner to the plight of slaves. Her friendship with Frances Gage at Hilton Head helped Barton to become more of a feminist and more of an advocate for black Americans. What she saw of the Massachusetts 54th Regiment, made up of black soldiers and white officers, convinced her of the nobility of the abolitionist cause and of the worthiness of blacks.

General Gilmore, who was only faintly aware of Barton and her efforts, planned his Fort Wagner attack well. Days of bombardment came first, days in which hundreds, if not thousands of shells hit the fort. Unknown to Gilmore and his Union soldiers, the Confederates were safely hunkered down in the central part of the fort. Although the bombardment was distressing, it did not cause many casualties. So, when the Union attacked on July 18, 1863, the enemy was ready.

The black soldiers of the Massachusetts 54th Regiment were the first in line and the first to attack. They crossed the sands, made blazing hot by the sun, only to be greeted by murderous rifle and cannon fire. It was yet another time when the Civil War showed the power of fighting on the defensive. The black troops fought bravely; some of them reached the ramparts and jumped into Fort Wagner, only to be shot and killed.

Colonel Elwell was unwell, having broken his leg weeks before. But from where he stood, near the center of the Union lines, the tension was unbearable. He jumped on a horse and galloped toward Fort Wagner, trying to rally the Union men even though they were not under his command. Reaching the fort, Elwell saw how hopeless the cause was, and he started riding back. Barton recognized her dear friend on horseback from about a mile away, but saw him fall about 150 yards (135 m) from the fort.

Running to him, Barton found the colonel badly wounded. He had crawled on hands and knees to safety, like a turtle, he later said, but she found him in poor condition. Barton spent days nursing Elwell, and, when it seemed he would mend, he was taken by ship to Hilton Head.

There were many other wounded to tend to, for the assault on Fort Wagner was a complete failure. Nearly 1,500 Union men were killed, wounded, or went missing that day. Barton reported a newfound admiration for the African-American soldiers, who she said were as gallant and uncomplaining as any she had encountered. She remained in the area for weeks, appalled by the misery she found.

A New Nation

Barton was 39 when the Civil War began and 43 when it ended. In those four years, she aged and her hair turned grey, but her spirit grew stronger. A photograph taken by Matthew Brady in 1865 shows the vigor and strength she had gained.

Barton returned to Hilton Head soon after the disastrous attack on Fort Wagner. She watched Colonel Elwell return to health, but their relationship was not what it had previously been. They became rather uncomfortable in each other's presence and sometimes avoided one another. Barton was also troubled with family difficulties. David had proved hopelessly incompetent as a quartermaster and was relieved of his position toward the end of 1863. Barton's favorite nephew, Irving Vassall (Sally's son), was slowly

A photo of Clara Barton by Mathew Brady, circa 1865. After her service on the battlefields during the Civil War, Barton assisted in identifying the remains of Union soldiers who died at the Confederate prison at Andersonville.

wasting away from tuberculosis. And there was still no news of her brother Stephen.

Barton returned to Washington at the beginning of 1864 in the lowest spirits she had felt for some time.

THE BATTLE WITH DIX

Dorothea Dix had, by this time, won the battle with Clara Barton over who should govern nursing work on the battle-field. Dix and Barton, who were so alike in their humanitarian spirit, did not like each other personally, and Barton had sought to avoid being trapped in Dix's corps of nurses. By the spring of 1864, Dix was firmly in control of the nurses, and it was all Barton could do to find some work of her own. Only the immediate need created by the Battle of the Wilderness and the Battle of Spotsylvania Courthouse brought Barton back to the front.

General Ulysses S. Grant, who had won fame in the western campaigns, came east in 1864 to fight Robert E. Lee and the Army of Northern Virginia. Unlike those generals who had gone before him, from McClellan to Burnside, Grant was a fighter who never gave up. He wanted to press the issue all the way to complete victory. Today, historians regard his efforts as the first attempt at *total war*—a war of unlimited scope, using all available resources in order to wipe out the enemy's ability to continue resisting. Knowing Grant's reputation for victory, Northerners were delighted when he took charge of the Union armies in March 1864 but were appalled by the casualty lists from his first two battles. More than 20,000 Northern men were killed, wounded, or missing in the battles of May 1864 alone.

Barton would still have been kept from the battlefield had she not won the admiration of yet another leading Union man. General Benjamin Butler from Massachusetts (known as "Beast" Butler to Southerners) gave her command of a small outpost of nurses with the Army of the James in the spring of 1864. Barton was there to minister to the wounded from the Battle of Cold Harbor, at which 8,000 men were killed, wounded, or went missing in a matter of one hour.

There were the all-too-familiar scenes of bandages missing and a lack of night lighting. There were desperate moments when nothing could be done for yet another soldier, and there were strange encounters when Barton met men who had once been schoolboys in her classrooms. Though she did her work as well as ever, something was missing from Barton at this time. The joy she had felt when accompanying the Army of the Potomac in 1862 was not present in her service with the Army of the James. Most of all, she was preoccupied with thoughts of her brother Stephen.

The word, when it arrived, was not good. When the war began, Stephen had been caught in the Confederacy and there had been no way for him to return to Massachusetts. Seeking to make the best of a bad situation, he had sold supplies of corn and gunpowder to both sides. The Confederates had warned him about continuing to do this, but it was actually his fellow Northerners who charged him with treason in 1864.

Nothing could harm Clara Barton more than an attack on her family name, and nothing would have distressed their now-deceased father more than to learn that his son and namesake was in federal prison. Barton appealed to General Butler, who agreed to have Stephen brought before him and court-martialed in the general's tent. The proceedings were probably illegal, from a military point of view, but Barton's earnest pleas to the general won the day. Stephen was released from custody.

Stephen was but a shadow of his former self. His weight had dropped from 200 pounds to 130 pounds (90 to 59 kilograms), and he could not stand without using a cane. Time spent in the federal prison had hurt his spirit and harmed his body. Having rescued so many other men from the edge, Barton turned all her attention to Stephen. She definitely improved his situation, but it was clear that his strength was fading fast.

In the winter of 1864 to 1865, the Army of Northern Virginia was on its last legs. It appeared only a matter of time before the Army of the Potomac captured Richmond, the capital of the Confederacy. But Barton had no time to celebrate, nor was she in a mood to do so. Stephen died in February and her beloved nephew died in March.

Barton managed the funerals and had her brother's body brought to Oxford. She had suffered through terrible losses during the Civil War. When the war began, the Bartons were one large, reasonably successful family, with only one member, Stephen, far from home. When it ended, Clara Barton was somewhat estranged from her brother David and his wife and she had lost her other brother and nephew. It was in the light of these tragedies that she confronted a tragedy for the nation: the assassination of Abraham Lincoln.

PASSING THE TORCH

Robert E. Lee surrendered the Army of Northern Virginia to Ulysses S. Grant on April 9, 1865. Barton was too occupied with grief over the recent deaths in her family to pay much attention to this, but she, like most Northerners, was greatly saddened by the assassination of Abraham Lincoln just five days later. Barton had met the president once or twice in passing, but her only memento was a short letter, written in his hand, one that showed her next course of action:

To the Friends of Missing Persons:

Miss Clara Barton has kindly offered to search for the missing prisoners of war. Please address her at Annapolis, giving the name, regiment, and company of any wounded prisoner.

(signed) A. Lincoln[1]

Barton had found a new cause: the location and identification of missing soldiers from the war.

ANDERSONVILLE

When the war ended, Barton learned that thousands of Northern men had died at an infamous Confederate prison in Andersonville, South Carolina. The prison superintendent had been more than cruel. The guards had been hateful toward their prisoners, many of whom had died after eating nothing more than grass. Locating and identifying the victims of Andersonville became one of the great passions of Barton's life. Barton was now entering a new phase. As she had always done, she threw herself into her new task.

A Connecticut man named Dorence Atwater who had been a prisoner at Andersonville had been charged by prison officials with keeping records of the sick, diseased, and dying men. He had drawn up the roster, and, fearing that the Confederates would take it from him before they were freed, he had made a duplicate. He presented the duplicate to Barton. Together, they called for the establishment of a proper cemetery at Andersonville.

Colonel Moore, the military commander assigned to the project, did not think very much of Barton, nor did she think much of him. They went by steamship from Washington to Savannah, and from there on to Andersonville by land. Though Barton had been on many

This sign was one of the many Civil War-era items discovered in the long-neglected attic of a commercial building in Washington where Clara Barton lived toward the end of the Civil War.

a battlefield and met many Southerners (some of whom she had tended and nursed), this trip to Andersonville was her first up-close and personal experience of the South. It did not wear well.

Arriving at Andersonville, Barton and the others were overcome by the stench of decaying bodies, and the filth that had piled up in nearby streams. Toward the end, the Confederate jailers had done almost nothing for the Yankee prisoners, who had died in huge numbers. Only a few former prisoners remained alive at Andersonville. The place seemed to charge the South with crimes of inhumanity.

Barton, Atwater, and their companions spent about two months at the former prison, during which time they identified thousands of shallow graves. (Atwater had been in charge of marking them with stakes.) Time and again, they succeeded in their cause, yet felt their efforts were not enough in the face of such overwhelming cruelty and neglect.

Barton's relationship with Colonel Moore continued to sour. It was clear that he viewed her as a useless female, full of feeling and empathy but lacking in any practical skills. Considering that much of her life had been dedicated to proving the opposite, Barton was angry. Her letters suggest that she came to look upon Colonel Moore as an enemy, though in fact he simply did not care about her and her cause.

When the last identifiable graves had been marked, Barton decided to go by train to Washington rather than return to the capital city with Colonel Moore. This was a mistake, for it took her off the scene at a time when she could have helped Atwater. When she returned to Washington, Barton found he had been charged with stealing Army property (the rosters) and that he was about to be court-martialed. Colonel Moore would be testifying for the prosecution. Barton had no authority to interfere in a court-martial, but she later obtained the court record (probably illegally) and found that Atwater had received a stiff fine and a sentence of 18 months in prison. Relieved to see that her name did not appear in the proceedings, Barton let the matter go. Three months later, Atwater and many other prisoners were released by the special order of President Andrew Johnson. Atwater soon came to live with Barton at her Washington house.

LECTURE CIRCUIT

Toward the end of 1865, Barton was at one of the lowest times of her adult life. She had finally been removed from the rolls of the U.S. Patent Office, so she had no work. Her funds were practically at an end; one record suggests she managed to live on about 50 cents a day. But all this was about to change.

In February 1866, Barton testified before Congress for the Joint Committee on Reconstruction. The representatives and senators on the committee had the difficult task of deciding how to bring the defeated Southern states back into the Union. Barton's appearance, however, was of a more personal nature: She sought to be paid back for money she had paid out of her own pocket during the Civil War.

Barton had never been a good keeper of receipts. Her life was too busy for that. What she presented to the committee were stories of how she had spent $12,000 of her own money, and about $3,000 from other sources. The committee leaders, not known to be soft and emotional, were nevertheless swayed by Barton's testimony. She received a full reimbursement of $15,000—a huge sum at the time. Because she was paid in government bonds rather than cash, Barton was able to live off the interest for years into the future. This was the closest she had ever come to genuine financial independence.

Barton then began a lecture tour that took her through many states in the North and Midwest over the next year and a half. At first she dreaded the experience, believing she had little skill for this kind of work, but her natural communication skills surfaced. Not only did she decorate her speeches with colorful descriptions of individual battles, but she also made many listeners—male and female alike—feel as if they had experienced some part of the Civil War. Though she never came to truly like giving speeches, Barton made an excellent living from it, charging between

$75 and $100 for each lecture. At times, she donated the proceeds to worthy causes, but there were plenty of occasions when she pocketed the entire amount.

At this time, Barton's health began to fail her. Having always been vigorous and strong, she tended to take her good health for granted. But, as had happened during her years as a teacher, her voice gave way. Some may have thought she was faking it in order to get out of giving more lectures, but anyone who came to her bedside during 1868 was convinced of her serious illness. Much of her hair fell out, and there were days when she could barely sit up.

Her physician prescribed a long period of complete rest. So long as she remained in Washington, she would forever be at the mercy of some new passion or calling, so he recommended she leave for an extended European vacation.

Red on White

Barton arrived in Scotland in the autumn of 1868, accompanied by her sister Sally Barton Vassall. Sally had come with Barton to provide company, but the agreement was that she would return to the United States as soon as Barton was settled in London. Once this was done, Sally went home on the next steamship, leaving Barton alone.

Alone! It might have been a magic word, had Barton been more used to it. Ever since the spring of 1861, when she first tended to Union soldiers, she had been in the thick of things, gathering supplies, distributing them, and tending to the wounded. Seldom had she enjoyed any privacy, let alone peace. But now, when she needed it most, Barton seemed unable to claim any peace for herself. Her restless spirit kept her on the go.

SWITZERLAND

By the winter she was in Switzerland, where she stayed with the family of a man she knew from Washington, D.C. The Golay family was delighted to have Barton in their home, but she felt out of sorts. She had seldom suffered from cold weather earlier in life, but now, in her late forties, she felt the cold deeply. Even worse was the fact that she had no way to make herself feel useful. Feeling at loose ends and suffering from the European cold, she fled to the island of Corsica. Emperor Napoleon Bonaparte had long been a hero of hers, and she wished to see his birthplace.

A few weeks of touring Corsica cured Barton of the desire. She saw some sights and enjoyed the warm island air, but other tourists, most of them English, snubbed her. After just a few months, Barton returned to Switzerland, where she had one of the greatest life-changing moments she had known.

THE RED CROSS

About a decade earlier, in June 1859, a Swiss businessman named Henri Dunant happened to be near the Battle of Solferino, fought between allied French and Italian forces and the Austrian army. About 40,000 men were killed or wounded on that frightful day. Dunant had nursed many of the wounded after the battle and had come away horrified by the brutality of modern war. Perhaps war had always been a terrible thing, he realized, but modern technology was making it worse.

Dunant later wrote an influential book on his experiences, *A Memory of Solferino*. It was an instant success, translated into numerous languages and became a guidepost for those who wished to create something better for the men on the battlefield. In 1863, Dunant and several of his supporters formed the International Committee for the Relief of the Wounded, the precursor to the International Committee of the Red Cross. A year later, at the urging of Dunant and two others Swiss leaders, an international meeting was set in Geneva for the summer of 1864, about the same time that Barton was tending the wounded soldiers of the battles of the Wilderness and Cold Harbor. The United States was not among the 12 nations that signed the Geneva Accords of August 1864. Although more nations soon signed on to the accord, the United States did not.

When asked why her country had not signed the accords, Barton had no answer. She had never heard of the Geneva Accords and had no idea why her native land had chosen not to enter the agreements. Barton immersed herself in the documents in Geneva. In all, 24 nations, including Russia, Turkey, France, England, and Spain, had ratified the document. She found nothing in the papers but good intentions, with the possibility of making people's lives better:

DID YOU KNOW?

THE GENEVA CONVENTIONS

In August 1864, 12 European nations voluntarily signed the first Geneva Accord, which ruled that ambulances, medical personnel, and other emergency aid workers should be considered as neutrals in any future conflict. In 1874, a second accord was reached, which broadened the definition of neutrality, and expanded the possibilities for the International Red Cross. Today, the Geneva Conventions consist of four treaties that set the standards for international law for humanitarian concerns. As of 2006, 194 countries have adopted and ratified the conventions.

Article I. Ambulances (field hospitals) and military hospitals shall be acknowledged to be neutral. . . .

Article II. Persons employed in hospitals and ambulances . . . shall participate in the benefit of neutrality. . . .

Article III. The persons designated in the preceding article may, even after occupation by the enemy, continue to fulfill their duties in the hospital or ambulance. . . .

Article IV. As the equipment of military hospitals remains subject to the laws of war, persons attached to such hospitals cannot, on withdrawing, carry away any articles but such as are their private property. . . .

Article V. Inhabitants of the country who may bring help to the wounded shall be respected and remain free. . . .

Article VI. Wounded or sick soldiers shall be entertained and taken care of, to whatever nation they may belong.

Article VII. A distinctive and uniform flag shall be adopted for hospitals, ambulances, and evacuations. It must on every occasion be accompanied by the national flag. . . .

Article VIII. The details of execution of the present convention shall be regulated by the commanders in chief of belligerent armies. . . .

Article IX. The high contracting powers have agreed to communicate the present convention to those governments which have not found it convenient to send [ambassadors to Geneva]. . . .

Article X. The present convention shall be ratified and the ratification shall be exchanged at Berne [Switzerland], in four months, or sooner if possible. . . .

Done at Geneva, the twenty-third day of August, 1864.[18]

Barton could see no reason whatsoever why the U.S. government had not signed the accords. Had her European stay ended at this point, Barton might have gone home with only a basic understanding of the accords and might have given up arguing the point. But fate stepped in: the Franco-Prussian War of 1870 to 1871.

SHIFTING POWERS

Napoleon I ruled as emperor of France from 1804 until 1814. His grandnephew Napoleon III ruled from 1851 until 1870. Under these two rulers, France was counted as the greatest of the European military powers. During the reign of Prussia's King Wilhelm I, however, Prussia became a strong competitor. In the summer of 1870, France declared war on Prussia.

To Barton, it meant little whether France or Prussia was in the right. What mattered was the suffering endured by thousands during the war. France and Prussia both employed new, modern weaponry, including the repeating rifle and the steel cannon. The casualty figures were terrifying.

Barton and a Swiss woman went to the front, armed with Red Cross bandages and flags (red crosses atop a white background, the opposite of the Swiss flag). They were seldom allowed to actually treat the men's battle wounds. Although both France and Prussia had signed the Geneva Accords, the soldiers of both nations routinely showed disrespect to anyone traveling under the Red Cross flag. One Prussian soldier, mistaking Barton for a barmaid, pinned her to a wall with his bayonet when she refused to serve him a drink.

Although she did not get to the front, Barton did minister to civilians on both sides. Given that Prussia successfully invaded France—rather than the other way around—it was Frenchmen and women who claimed the bulk of her attention. Barton was especially active in and around Strasbourg, which had held out for two months before yielding to the Prussians. Barton held no official role until Louise, the Grand Duchess of Baden (a German principality), was won over by Barton's personality and her mission. The duchess gave generously from her own purse to assist Barton in helping the people of Strasbourg. Typically, Barton did not think simple handouts would do. She believed that the townspeople needed to work to regain their self-respect. Soon, she had a set of circles of women, busily sewing garments for rich and poor alike.

When her work in Strasbourg was completed, Barton went to the frontier areas of Alsace and Lorraine, two provinces that had been under French rule until the war. She found the peasants dirty, unkempt, and ignorant and later confessed that she had "no French" in her soul. She found Germans much more likeable. As little as she liked the frontier work, Paris proved even more difficult. The city was in complete disarray, both from the Prussian siege of four months, and from the recent conflict between the "Communards" (the forerunners of Communists) and the Parisian police.

EXAGGERATING THE RECORD

Up to this point in life, Barton had maintained a largely truthful record of her accomplishments. When she lectured to U.S. audiences about the Civil War, she sometimes made things seem grander than they were, but she did not lie. This was not the case when it came to her work in France.

Fearing that anything less than drama would fail to get supplies and money from people around the world, Barton exaggerated her experiences in the Franco-Prussian War. People who read her letters and pamphlets about the war would never have guessed that she had not been allowed to reach the front, or that she had lain in bed a good deal of her time in Paris, suffering from nervous exhaustion. One

(continues on page 72)

Florence Nightingale, the revolutionary nurse, author, and statistician, who came to be known as "The Lady with the Lamp."

THE CLARA BARTON OF ENGLAND

Almost from the beginning of her Civil War work, Barton had been called the "Florence Nightingale of America." The title did not please her, as it tended to put her second to the great English nurse. In truth, however, there were some striking similarities between the two women.

Born in Florence, Italy, on May 12, 1820, a year and a half before Barton, Nightingale came from a well-to-do British family that enjoyed excellent social connections. She responded to a religious calling at the age of 16, believing she was meant to nurse the poor and sick. This decision caused her family much distress, but she went right ahead. In this, as in other ways, she was much like Barton.

Nightingale came to fame during the Crimean War of 1851 to 1854, which was fought between the British, French, and Turks on one side, and the Russians on the other. She spent months in Crimean hospitals, tending to men who might otherwise have withered and died. Today, it seems unbelievable that a rich and powerful country such as Britain would not have an effective army hospital service, but this was the case until Nightingale shamed the British government through her actions.

Known as "The Lady with the Lamp" (like Barton, she believed in good hygiene and good lighting), Nightingale was invited by Queen Victoria to lead a royal commission on finding ways to improve army hospitals. Her fame only increased throughout life, and she was, next to Victoria, the most famous of British women of her time.

Florence and Barton never met. They were in London at the same time, in 1872. They politely sent letters to each other and each used poor health as an excuse to avoid personal contact with the other. Florence Nightingale died in 1910 at the age of 90.

(continued from page 69)

of her devoted co-workers was appalled to find that Barton wrote they had met a trainload of returning soldiers on a day when both women were ill.

It is ironic that Barton started to exaggerate at this point in life, for she was finally beginning to achieve serious recognition. Her countrymen had known little of her until she undertook her lecture series, and the European public knew even less. But her actions on the Franco-Prussian border and in Paris won her many admirers. By the end of 1872, she could count the Grand Duchess Louise and Kaiser Wilhelm I (the war had elevated him from King of Prussia to Emperor of Germany), as well as Count Bismarck of Prussia among her correspondents. Kaiser Wilhelm was so impressed with Barton and her work that he awarded her the German Iron Cross.

Barton was exhausted. Having done so much in the war and so much for the people of Paris in the aftermath, she was again on the verge of serious illness. So she left Paris for London, to rest.

London welcomed Barton. She was invited to numerous teas and luncheons, and she became, perhaps, one of the best-known American women in the British capital city. But her health did not improve. In fact, it worsened, perhaps because of the dampness in the air. While in London, she spent much of her time in bed.

HOME AGAIN

By 1872, Barton was longing for home. She wished to be among Americans again. Midway across the Atlantic onboard the steamship *Parthia*, she penned a poem:

> Have ye place, each beloved one, a place in your prayer,
> Have ye room, my dear countrymen, room for me there?[2]

Did Barton mean the Red Cross? Did she despair of convincing her countrymen of its importance? Or was she concerned for herself? By this time in life, it was hard to tell the difference, for she and her cause had become almost tangled into one.

To the Rescue

Barton's fifty-second birthday approached as she returned from Europe. Although many people of her age and era would have felt they had done enough in life, Barton came from a long-lived family and expected to be in the field for many years to come.

ANOTHER LOSS

During the four years she was abroad, Barton wrote home to her sister, nephews, and cousins in Oxford frequently. Only upon coming back to Massachusetts did she realize that her sister Sally's health had worsened during her absence. By the time Barton returned, it was clear that Sally had stomach cancer.

Barton had been of great assistance to soldiers in the field, but she was unable to do much for her sister. Because she now suffered greatly in severe cold, Barton moved south to Washington, thinking that the southerly location would do her good. Instead, she suffered a full nervous collapse and was in a Washington hospital when she learned her sister's condition had worsened. Barton was unable to make the trip back to Oxford. When she finally did, she arrived at Oxford about 10 hours too late. Sally, her last connection with the older generation of female Bartons, was gone. It was enough to put Barton in the worst condition of her life.

INVALID YEARS

For the next two years, Barton was a true invalid. She lived first with family in Oxford and then moved in with cousins in nearby Grafton. She could walk only a few paces at a time, and her hair, which had long been a source of vanity, fell out. She became irritable and short-tempered. Neighbors came to visit her but often left feeling ignored. Even little children—upon whom Barton had always lavished attention—felt that she was not as friendly as before. Eventually, Barton turned to the only thing that offered hope: time at a sanitarium.

The institution in Dansville, New York, was not strictly for mentally ill patients, but rather it embraced a holistic approach to health. It offered its clients peace, rest, and gentle stimulation through music and lectures. A number of prominent persons had already been at Dansville, but Barton was probably the best known to attend in the 1870s.

Barton was unused to a soothing routine of wholesome food and gentle relaxation. Each time she had previously tried this, she had failed to quiet her restless spirit. Yet, something about the Dansville staff enabled her to stay, and to thrive. Within six months, she was writing cheerful letters home about Dansville and its staff.

The town was another matter. After the stimulation she had felt in Europe, Barton felt closed in by what she considered to be simple, country attitudes. But Dansville proved to be the perfect place from which to launch her next cause: adoption of the Geneva Accords by the U.S. government.

TELLING THE STORY

About a year after she left Dansville, Barton wrote to the Swiss gentlemen she had known, asking if she might be of assistance in trying to win U.S. acceptance of the Geneva Accords. When these gentlemen responded positively, Barton asked them to authorize her as their sole representative in the United States. This, too, was agreed upon, and Barton then entered into one of the most difficult—and ultimately rewarding—struggles of her life.

Since 1796, the year that President George Washington issued his Farewell Address, Americans had generally believed in the principle of friendship toward all nations and "entangling alliances" with none. The Monroe Doctrine of 1823 had pressed the point even further, warning the nations of Europe to keep out of the Western Hemisphere. It made sense, therefore, that U.S. policymakers were reluctant to agree to anything that might tie their hands or force their behavior.

Luckily, Barton had allies. She went first to President James Garfield, who politely referred her to the secretary of state, James Blaine. A fellow New Englander, Blaine was quite pleased with the idea of joining the Geneva Accords. When Barton told him there were objections based on the Monroe Doctrine, he brushed that aside. The Monroe Doctrine was not meant to cut the United States off from the rest of humanity, he said. The secretary promised to work for the passage of the Geneva Accords.

From there it was on to the office of Robert Todd Lincoln, the secretary of war and the son of the former president. After Barton pressed him on the matter, he confessed that he saw no reason why the Geneva Accords should not be adopted. Success seemed at hand.

There was, indeed, no objection at the highest levels of government, but the Senate had many other matters to attend to, and Barton's frequent raising of the issue sometimes irritated some members of that body. She might have succeeded sooner, had President Garfield not been cut down by an assassin's bullet in September 1881. Garfield lingered for some weeks but then died, and the presidency passed to Vice President Chester A. Arthur. The Senate then had much more important business, and Barton had to wait all over again. Although progress on the Geneva Accords was slow, Barton established the American Red Cross in 1881 while patiently waiting for an answer from the government.

There were times when it seemed that all her work had been for nothing, but finally, in the spring of 1883, the U.S. Senate unanimously agreed to the Geneva Accords. Copies of the treaty were bound, signed, and sealed, and Barton had a short look at them before they were sent to Geneva. Her greatest desire was, at last, fulfilled.

SHERBORN

In the autumn of 1884, Barton received an offer to become the temporary superintendent of the Massachusetts prison for women in Sherborn. The pay was just $1,500 per year and the hours would be long. Barton was interested only because the offer came from her old friend, the former Civil War General Benjamin Butler, who was now governor of Massachusetts. Barton, recalling what Butler had done for her and her nurses in 1864 to 1865, felt she could not refuse.

She went to Massachusetts and took up residence at the Women's Reformatory in Sherborn. There were about 40 other women on staff, ranging from guards to chaplains and housekeepers. There were about 300 prisoners, whose crimes ranged from minor offenses like pick pocketing to more serious ones. About half of all the women at Sherborn suffered from alcoholism.

The person who had held Barton's job before her had done great things in terms of living conditions at the prison. Critics of Sherborn complained that the inmates slept on better beds and ate better food than the average mill worker and his family. Barton agreed with many, if not most, of the things done by the old superintendent, and her changes were mostly ones of tone, rather than policy. For example, she had letterboxes installed so every inmate could write confidentially either to her or to the Massachusetts prison board. Although she had only infrequent contact with the inmates, Barton soon won their affection. To witnesses, it seemed she had an unmistakable gift for soothing and calming those in distress. Many of the inmates had heard of Barton's Civil War experiences. In her they found a worthy heroine.

The drawback was the loneliness. Barton had been in difficult positions many times before, but she had usually enjoyed the companionship of others. There had been chaplains, surgeons, and fellow nurses during the Civil War. In France and Prussia, she had been accompanied by two young women who adored her. At Sherborn, Barton suffered from the loneliness that came with her position of leadership. Then, too, she was bothered with almost never-ending correspondence: She had to report to Governor Butler, to the Massachusetts prison board, and she had to reply to questions posed by local newspapers. On top of all this, Barton still tried to run the American Red Cross from afar.

It was all too much, and she sometimes felt near the breaking point. When Governor Butler lost his bid for reelection in November 1883, she handed in her resignation. He convinced her to remain until the beginning of the New Year, but when she walked out of Sherborn, she ceased all connection with the institution. It was as if she felt too deeply the pains and sufferings of the inmates; it was too uncomfortable for her to be near them.

Even so, the time at Sherborn marked a major change in Barton's life. Throughout her life, she had identified primarily with men, seeking their company (whether they were generals, privates, or doctors) and enjoying the compliments she received. Perhaps Barton had already begun to shift before arriving at Sherborn, but by the time she left, she was definitely committed to making the world a better place for women.

DISASTER RELIEF

Almost from the beginning, Barton had understood that the Red Cross could be useful in domestic emergencies. The Red Cross founders in Switzerland had imagined the organization to be most useful in wartime, but Barton had in mind the kinds of natural events that could disrupt daily living in the United States. In 1884, she had her first big opportunity to show what the Red Cross could do during such a situation.

The Ohio River flooded on a regular basis, but the floods of 1884 were something quite out of the ordinary. Upon hearing of the flood, Barton went west, and along with Dr. Julian Hubbell she floated down the Ohio on a steamboat called the *Josh V. Throop*. Together, they distributed supplies of food and clothing to the needy.

This first major American Red Cross operation was a decided success, but Barton continued to experience conflict and difficulty. This time it was with independent

Red Cross branches that set up operation without first consulting with the national organization. New York City's large population allowed it to establish a large citywide Red

BARTON AND THE SUFFRAGISTS

Barton first met Susan B. Anthony on a train ride in 1869. The two women had much in common: Both came from Massachusetts mill towns, and both had struggled mightily on the way to finding their identity and place in society. They became fast friends, a friendship that endured until their deaths.

By the 1880s, Susan B. Anthony and Elizabeth Cady Stanton were on a great crusade to win for women the right to vote. The first breakthroughs came not in the populated eastern states, but in western ones: Montana and Wyoming were far ahead of New York and Massachusetts, for example. Anthony, Stanton, and others waged a nonstop war against the denial of women's right to vote.

Barton completely agreed with Anthony and Stanton. To her, it was obvious that women should enjoy equal rights. Yet, as much as she agreed with the feminists, Barton never joined their ranks. Had she lent her name more forcefully to the cause, it might have advanced more rapidly, but her own Red Cross work might have suffered.

Barton did not live long enough to see women vote on a nationwide basis (that came in 1920), but by the time of her death in 1912, American women were making strides in all sorts of areas. When she visited Turkey in 1896 and Romania in 1897, Barton was appalled to see women pulling carts in the manner of horses. Trips such as these brought home to her the reality that American women were much more fortunate than many of their foreign counterparts.

Cross, and Barton soon found herself having to defend the original charter of the American Red Cross.

The Red Cross's many successes that followed were often marred by conflict and misunderstanding. Barton was certainly correct in believing that she possessed the original charter, but with some good will she might have secured the cooperation of other branches. Instead, she set her face and that of the American Red Cross against them.

As the 1880s drew to a close and Barton neared her seventieth birthday, she had much about which to feel pleased. As always, however, she was concerned over money. She had always been rather careless about receipts, and the problem was about to become worse. At the same time, though, she was headed for some of her greatest triumphs.

TO THE RESCUE

The single worst flood of U.S. history hit Johnstown, Pennsylvania, on May 31, 1889. For days there had been heavy rain, which had swollen the two nearby rivers, but on the last day of May, a major dam gave way, sending roughly 20 million tons of water downstream. Even Americans accustomed to weather extremes of drought, warmth, and excessive cold were stunned by the news from Johnstown. About 5,000 people died either on May 31 or in the three days that followed.

Like almost everyone else in Washington, D.C., Barton found it difficult to believe what she heard. Never before had one climatic event caused so much devastation. Within days, she was on a train headed for Johnstown. Upon arrival, she found conditions worse than those described in the reports. Many people were missing or dead. Most of the town's buildings were either swept away or difficult to recognize, for the oncoming water had tossed beams of wood around as if they were cardboard.

An illustration of Clara Barton that details her battlefield work during the Civil War and her efforts in organizing the American Red Cross. Note the banner of the Red Cross in the upper left corner.

Barton went straight to the military commander on the scene and was insulted to find he had never heard of the American Red Cross, much less the organization in Geneva. Still, he allowed her and about a dozen Red Cross workers to enter the scene of devastation, and Barton went to work. She had always believed that charity itself was not enough; indeed, that it led to a loss of spirit among the people who received it. But in this circumstance, she could offer little but charity. Red Cross shelters were set up, and within a month there were four newly constructed log structures to house many of the displaced.

Food and drink were just as pressing concerns as housing. True to her principles, Barton at first helped those in need find work so they could earn their food, but there were many occasions where food simply needed to be handed out. Donations came in from different parts of the country. One well-intentioned shoe manufacturer sent 6,000 pairs of shoes, but when Barton and her workers opened the cartons they found that all were for the left foot. Other donations were more useful, such as pine logs that came from a construction firm in Indiana.

Barton, Dr. Hubbell, and her company worked for three months at Johnstown, making a deep impression on the people of that stricken place. When they left in mid-autumn, the people penned all sorts of tributes to Barton personally and the Red Cross in general. The overall feeling was that she and the Red Cross had stepped in where no one else had even tried. That might be an exaggeration, but there would be another occasion on which it was all too true.

SOUTH SEA ISLANDS

In 1891, Barton and her associates renamed the American Red Cross as the American National Red Cross. This effort put Barton in touch with many people interested in charity and well-to-do men of business, some of whom would become major donors in the future. But, as usual, she was bedeviled with problems.

First there was a questionable gift of land in Indiana. The husband and wife who gave 960 acres (388 hectares) to Barton did so with the intention that the land would be used for establishing a Red Cross haven in the Midwest. But no sooner had she taken possession than Barton learned there were unpaid property taxes and other financial requirements. As she had often done, Barton pulled from her own large savings to make good the debt, but this was becoming a troubling pattern. There was also a growing problem within the national Red Cross ranks: Some members thought the organization would be better off without its founder.

An emergency arose to divert Barton's attention from her pressing difficulties. The South Sea Islands, which lie off the coasts of South Carolina and Georgia, were not new to Barton. She had been at Hilton Head during the Civil War. But she, like most Americans, was astonished to learn of the devastation caused by a hurricane in the summer of 1893.

U.S. newspapers and magazines reported on the wreckage of homes and plantations, but the average American simply shrugged at the crisis. Much of this had to do with racial stereotypes, since the island was home to a large population of African Americans. Many white Americans believed that blacks were naturally lazy and would never work so long as free food was available. The 30 years that had followed the Civil War had been unkind to African Americans, who had experienced a great deal of this prejudice. When Barton announced that the Red Cross would go to the scene, she was met with skepticism from many people.

DID YOU KNOW?

THE PROGRESSIVES

Barton was ahead of her time in many ways. As a young adult, she had dreamed of making a better world, and as a middle-aged woman she had done more than her share to make it possible. What could hurt more, therefore, than to learn that many younger women thought she held back the work of the Red Cross?

Born in 1821, Barton came from a time and place where women had few options. Though she often spoke poorly of her education, she had received a better one than many of her generation, and she was able to add to it throughout her life. During the Civil War era, American women still had few opportunities. But a new generation was emerging, one that Barton would feel was most ungrateful to her.

The Progressive Era emerged in the 1890s. Young to middle-aged women, quite a few of them graduates of new all-female colleges including Mount Holyoke and Smith, came to cities such as New York and Chicago. They were determined to improve the world, as Barton had been before them. The major difference between these women and Barton was income: Many of the new female Progressives came from families of means and many had college educations; some possessed advanced degrees. It was natural that Barton would feel ill at ease with these women, but not so predictable that some of them would turn on her.

Mabel T. Boardman personified this generation of women. With moderate wealth but great social connections, she was in a position to make Barton's life difficult. Had Barton resigned in the 1890s, or gotten out of the way in some respect, there might not have been a clash. Instead, destiny marked these two women out as rivals.

Earlier in life, Barton might have agreed with some of the stereotypes, but her great mentor Frances Gage had long since cured her of them. Gathering up her followers and some supplies, Barton rushed to the South Sea Islands. Black people on the islands had heard of Barton, and a few even remembered her from Civil War days.

Barton designed a system under which only families that planted new gardens (preferably with green vegetables) would receive food assistance, and she also managed to deliver some short-cotton seed for them to use. Typically, she saw charity as a waste unless it helped people help themselves.

Three months of work in the South Sea Islands provided one of the greatest satisfactions of Barton's life. The few reporters who did come south to see the Red Cross in action were enormously impressed. One wrote that the seeming lack of formal rules and regulations suggested that everything was actually running smoothly. Barton managed to hide her own bodily aches and pains (she was now 73) and appeared as active and spry as ever. Most touching was the way the islanders responded to her. When she left, a large group of people gathered around her and praised her as if she were their savior.

It was as close to true as it would ever be. The relief work in the South Sea Islands was one of Barton's finest moments.

Working Overseas

In 1894, Americans became aware of a new and bloody conflict overseas between the Ottoman Turks and the Christian Armenians. This was a long-standing struggle, with the Turks usually gaining the upper hand. The Ottoman Empire was in disarray in the 1890s, and some of its leaders used the confusion to find a scapegoat; namely, the Armenians.

Throughout 1894, Barton and other Red Cross leaders heard of the savagery of the fighting and, worse, of the inhumanity shown to Armenian civilians. At first, Barton doubted that she, the Red Cross, or anyone else could make much of a difference. Over time, however, pressure built in Washington for someone to do something.

Barton sailed from New York City in January 1896. She reached London easily enough, but there was a long holdup while diplomats from England, the United States, and the Ottoman Empire discussed how to "place" the Red Cross. Finally, in February, Barton and a handful of associates traveled to the Ottoman capital of Constantinople via the famed Orient Express, the train that carried travelers from one side of Europe to the other.

Upon arriving in Constantinople (known today as Istanbul), Barton had a meeting with one of the leading officials of the Ottoman Empire. The official, called a pasha, approved of the spirit of Barton's work, since the Ottomans had signed the Geneva Conventions, but he insisted that what she did in Turkey must be in her name alone, not in the name of the Red Cross.

This was the type of interference or difficulty Barton had met so many times in life, leaving her to carry the responsibility alone. She may well have wished to turn and go back at that very moment, but she accepted the pasha's requirement and went to work. Barton remained in Constantinople while four missions were sent to the Armenians in the countryside. This was a wise decision, for Barton, at 74, was not as spry as in the past. She learned to her horror that typhus was spreading through the Armenian communities, and she arranged to send doctors and nurses to the battlefront. It was a very small step compared to the needs of the moment.

Even worse, Barton began to receive strong criticism from people at home. The American National Red Cross was on the scene, doing work, but the New York Red Cross (still a separate organization) had actually raised more funds than Barton and her group. When it became clear that Barton was still the one really handing out money, the New York Red Cross and other humanitarian groups cut off further help for the American Red Cross. First annoyed, then furious, Barton cabled home that she and her group would proceed without any help whatsoever. And so they did.

Five months after arriving in Constantinople, and after having distributed food and items valued at $116,000, Barton headed for home. In many ways, the venture to Constantinople had been difficult, but she was delighted to receive, via the U.S. State Department, a heavy, jewel-encrusted medal, the Second Order of Shekafet, from the Ottoman Turkish sultan. As with so many other medals and honors received by Barton, it was the first time it had been issued to a woman.

THE SPANISH-AMERICAN WAR

In 1897, Barton felt the need for a long rest. Though to her staff she seemed tireless, friends and family members sometimes worried about how weary she seemed. It had been 32 years since the Civil War, and much of that time had been spent in the active building of the American Red Cross, or the defense of the same. If ever Barton needed and deserved time off, this was the moment, but it was not to be. Yet another crisis loomed.

Cuba lies just 90 miles (145 km) south of Key West, Florida, so it was natural that the United States would be interested in what went on there. American companies had invested heavily in Cuban sugar over the past three decades. So it was with concern, and a bit of alarm, that Americans learned that Cubans had begun a revolt against their Spanish colonial leaders.

What began as a fight between native Cubans and Spanish-born immigrants and creoles (a mixture of the two) erupted into a full-scale revolution. Spain sent nearly 200,000 soldiers to subdue the island, and throughout 1897, Americans heard tales of atrocities committed by both sides. Because the Spanish military had the upper hand, its actions received much more notice. Through newspapers such as the *New York World* and the *New York Times*, Americans learned that thousands of Cubans had been placed in concentration camps.

Barton was as up to date as any American when it came to Cuba, but she shuddered at the idea of getting involved with another international action. The Turkish-Armenian affair had been difficult enough. It was only through the action of President William McKinley that the Red Cross entered the Cuban situation. (McKinley was one of Barton's great admirers and a fellow veteran of the Battle of Antietam.) McKinley helped form the Central Cuban Relief Committee (CCRC), made up of individuals from the Red Cross and other groups, but he personally asked Barton to go to Cuba. On February 9, 1898, Barton landed in the harbor of Havana.

REMEMBER THE MAINE!

On the evening of February 15, Barton and an associate were laboring over paperwork in a Havana hotel. Suddenly, the windows blew open and the papers were scattered everywhere as an enormous explosion shook the harbor. Within minutes, Barton learned that the USS *Maine*, a battleship sent to protect U.S. interests, had been blown up. An hour later, she was at Ambrosia Hospital, where the 40-odd survivors had been taken. Barton went up and down the lines of men, ministering to them as she had to soldiers of the Civil War, but she also made careful notes about the type and quality of their wounds. (She correctly suspected there would be an investigation as to how the *Maine* had blown up). Sometime that night, she managed to send a telegram to President McKinley, with the dramatic words, "I am with the wounded."[1]

The president received her message that night, among a score of others. The thing he had most dreaded was upon him: war. McKinley had tried to hold off the call for war as long as he could, but the press, which had been fanning the flames of war with propaganda stories about oppressed Cubans, had turned most Americans decisively in favor of intervention in Cuba.

Americans mostly responded to the call "Remember the Maine!" but there were some who chose to remember the words "I am with the wounded." Barton's words were made into a popular poem:

> "I am with the wounded," flashed along the wire
> From the Isle of Cuba, swept with sword and fire.
> Angel sweet of mercy, may your cross of red
> Cheer the wounded living; bless the wounded dead.
>
> "I am with the starving," let the message run
> From this stricken island, when this task is done;
> Food and plenty wait at your command,
> Give in generous measure; fill each outstretched hand.
>
> "I am with the happy," this we long to hear
> From the Isle of Cuba, trembling now in fear;
> Make this great disaster touch the hearts of men,
> And, in God's great mercy, bring back peace again.[2]

By the time the United States declared war on Spain on April 21, 1898, Barton and about 30 Red Cross personnel were in Tampa, Florida, awaiting an opportunity to cross to Cuba. Barton was aboard the supply ship *State of Texas*, with 1,400 tons (1,270 metric tons) of supplies ranging from emergency kits to tools. But she, like other rescue workers, had to wait.

The U.S. Army, small until the declaration of war, had named Tampa its point of departure. There were thousands of soldiers in Tampa, some of the old military type and some very young men who had never fired a shot in anger.

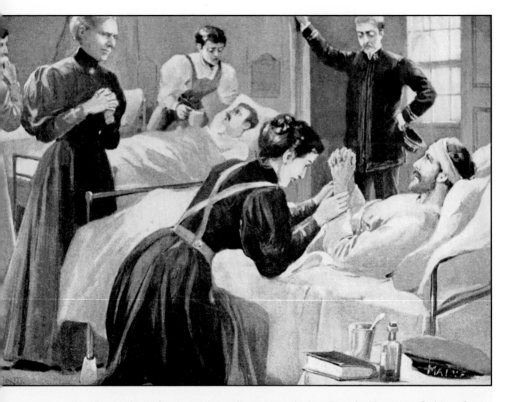

An illustration of nurses attending wounded sailors in Havana, Cuba, after the explosion of the USS *Maine* in 1898.

Barton, the Red Cross, and all other rescue efforts had to wait until about 14,000 men were embarked and steaming toward Cuba.

The Spanish-American War was not a costly conflict, especially by Civil War standards, but it was the first major engagement fought by the U.S. military since 1865, and many young men wanted their share of the glory. Theodore Roosevelt, who at 40 years old had resigned as assistant secretary of the U.S. Navy, was one of these. While Barton and her rescue workers waited at Tampa, Roosevelt and his regiment of cavalry volunteers, dubbed the "Rough Riders," steamed off for Cuba.

TO THE RESCUE

Barton and her associates had to wait almost two weeks before departing for Cuba. As they approached the southeastern side of the island, near the major city of Santiago de Cuba, Barton wrote: "It is to the Rough Riders that we go, and the relief may be also rough but it will be ready."[3] The prospect of directly caring for wounded men sparked something in her soul, something that had not been fully lit since the end of the Civil War. This was the work that her father had charged her to do, on his deathbed, back in 1862.

The U.S. Army descended from its ships at Siboney, where it experienced little resistance and only a few casualties. From there, however, it was a very rough road, through nearly jungle-like conditions, to Santiago de Cuba. Barton and her associates came off the *State of Texas* and followed the army inland. At first they had just a few men to help, often those who had come down with malaria or dysentery. But as the U.S. Army neared Santiago, the Spanish resistance grew stronger. On July 1, 1898, the two sides fought at the Battle of San Juan Hill.

On that hot, steamy day, Colonel Theodore Roosevelt led the Rough Riders forward in a gallant but extremely risky attack on San Juan Hill. Two regiments of African-American soldiers also participated. Leading the charge, Roosevelt brought his men up Kettle Hill (where the battle was actually fought), to seize the commanding heights overlooking Santiago. In so doing he practically ensured that the U.S. Army would capture that city. But the army's success of that day was entirely spoiled for Barton and the Red Cross workers, who helped hundreds of dead and wounded.

The battlefield and the Red Cross camp a few miles below were a terrible sight. The new rapid-fire rifles, produced both in Spain and the United States, had created a death scene that Barton had seldom encountered. It is true that the casualties at the Battle of Antietam, 30 years earlier, were far greater than those at the Battle of San Juan Hill. Still, San Juan Hill left a memory just as deep and emotional for Barton.

Most unhappily of all, Barton was able to witness how little medical supplies and equipment had changed since the Civil War. To friends and associates she remarked bitterly that it was as if all her work of the previous 35 years had been for nothing. The U.S. Army of 1898 was no better equipped to bring back its wounded, or to tend to them, than the Union Army had been in 1862.

Barton worked 16-hour days in the aftermath of the Battle of San Juan Hill. To the men on the ground—lying on stretchers or being carried to the surgeon's table—she was a living legend: the Angel of the Battlefield returned, to care for the wounded once more. But to surgeons, captains, and majors, she often seemed in the way. They believed that the Army could take care of its own, without the help of Barton and her nurses, decked out in neatly starched uniforms.

They were wrong.

The days after the Battle of San Juan Hill proved that Barton had not outlived her usefulness—there was as much of a need for her services, and those of the Red Cross, as ever. One could argue—and many did—that the Red Cross needed younger leadership, but Barton remained an inspiring example. One of the most touching stories from this time is an encounter between Colonel Theodore Roosevelt and Barton.

Roosevelt came to the Red Cross camp to ask for medical supplies for his men. He offered to pay for them, to which Barton responded they were not for sale. Impatient and concerned, Roosevelt expressed how great the need was. Barton then replied that nothing in the Red Cross camp was for sale, but he could have it all for free if he simply asked. She soon loaded up Colonel Roosevelt with a sack full of medical supplies.

Clara Barton (*front row, sixth from left*) and fellow Red Cross workers gather on a dock in Cuba during the Spanish-American War.

Barton failed in only one matter, but it was important. Yellow fever became epidemic in the U.S. Army camps after the Battle of San Juan Hill, and Barton decided to keep the *State of Texas* out of reach of the contagious disease. No wounded soldiers could go aboard the ship, and the Red Cross nurses were, temporarily, kept back from the U.S. Army camps. This was a disastrous decision, one that cost Barton much of the good will she had previously created. Her personal secretary, George Kennan, resigned from the Red Cross in protest.

The Spanish surrendered Santiago two weeks after the battle. On the day that the U.S. fleet was to enter Santiago Harbor, Barton loaded up the *State of Texas* and had everything ready, when she learned the astonishing news that Admiral William T. Sampson had decided to let the Red Cross be the first in line. Later she expressed her feelings as she discovered that her little steamship was the only one heading up the channel to the docks:

> Are we really going into Santiago—and alone? . . . Could it be possible that the commander who had captured a city declined to be the first to enter—that he would hold back his flagship and himself and send forward, and first, a cargo of food on a plain ship, under the direction of a woman? Did our commands, military or naval, hold men great enough of soul for such action?[4]

True it was. Clara Barton and the Red Cross were first ashore.

Last Battles

U ntil 1898, Barton had very much run the Red Cross as if it were her own. Indeed, she sometimes referred to it as "my baby." But by 1900, a small but determined group of opponents had risen within Red Cross ranks. They could not be ignored.

Chief among them was Mabel T. Boardman. About 40 at the time, she came from a well-connected family. She knew President McKinley, as well as the leaders of many U.S. corporations. Under other circumstances, she and Barton might have been allies, but Boardman saw it as her task to push Barton from her Red Cross leadership and to bring the American Red Cross into the modern era.

Barton had three triumphs left to enjoy before her resignation. First, on June 6, 1900, a bill passed through the U.S. Congress formally incorporating the American National Red Cross. Barton had argued for this for many years, thinking that only the protection of the U.S. government could ensure that Red Cross symbols were used only by the organization and not by anyone looking to make a quick buck from the organization's name. Although the protection was limited, at least there were no more "Red Cross ketchup" and "Red Cross shoes."

Barton also attended the seventh conference of the International Red Cross in St. Petersburg, Russia, in May 1902. There, she received the lavish attention of foreign dignitaries, including Czar Nicholas II and Czarina Alexandra. This was exactly the type of praise Barton occasionally lacked in her homeland. Suspecting that this would be her last overseas trip, Barton visited her old patroness, Louise, the Grand Duchess of Baden, who told her, "Tell them in America how I love you."

On her return, Barton saw that the American National Red Cross was split into two groups of opinion. There were men and women who had stuck with her through thick and thin, and there were the opponents, mainly younger men and women who had not served with Barton in the field. If Barton had maintained the good will of people like her former secretary, George Kennan, her chances of weathering this storm would have been better. Even as things were, Barton managed one last triumph.

By writing to some people beforehand and gaining their proxies (the right to vote on their behalf), Barton managed to have things her way at the annual Red Cross meeting. Not only were her expense requests approved, she was also voted president for life. This was an astonishing victory, but it was her last.

Just a month later, Theodore Roosevelt, who had since become the twenty-sixth president of the United States, wrote a cold, sharp letter severing his relationship with the

Red Cross. As president, Roosevelt was head of the Red Cross board of directors, and his abrupt move took Barton and her associates by surprise. Later, they found that Mabel T. Boardman and her associates had asked the president for this move.

The president's removal of his support put the Red Cross into an emergency situation, where it had to fight for its own survival. Barton found herself and her management of funds the subject of a congressional investigation, headed by Senator Redfield Proctor. Those who knew Barton well laughed at the very idea that she had ever steered Red Cross funds in her own direction. At the age of 80, she lived as simply and as inexpensively as she had at 40 or even 20. But critics abounded, and there was some truth to their charges that Barton, as founder, had *become* the Red Cross. Donations from individuals and businesses had been sloppily accepted, without enough of a paper trail for one to follow. There was also some truth that the Red Cross had failed to set up measures of accountability, leaving most of the power in the hands of one person.

In personal matters, Barton was forgiving of the excesses or errors of her associates. Therefore, she was deeply pained by the investigation and its finger-pointing, most of it aimed in her direction. One of the most painful moments came when a former Red Cross employee testified that Barton had accepted a deed of land in Indiana for her own benefit, rather than that of the organization. The land was in Barton's name, but to claim she had ever benefited from the situation was laughable. Rather, she had shelled out much of her own money to keep it. On the day when Barton's lawyer would have had his opportunity to cross-examine this key witness, the person fled Washington. Upon learning of this, Senator Proctor announced the investigation closed, with Barton completely exonerated.

It was one more victory, but it was largely hollow. Barton knew that her opponents in the Red Cross would dig up other matters, examining every donation she had ever accepted and every bill she had ever paid from Red Cross funds. Soon after having her name cleared, Barton turned in her letter of resignation as Red Cross president, effective on May 14, 1904.

She had been president for 22 years and had served as the energy behind the organization's creation for a dozen years before that. Barton was now 83, and friends naturally wondered if she would ever retire.

LAST YEARS

Barton was distressed, even sullen, over the loss of the presidency. Reporters who visited her at Glen Echo, Maryland, over the next few years found her happy to discuss almost any subject except the Red Cross, which had passed the leadership to Mabel T. Boardman. Barton had one last project in her, however: the furthering of a National First Aid Society.

First Aid and the Red Cross are now nearly synonyms, so much so that it is difficult to think of a time when they were two separate organizations. The National First Aid Society had Barton as its president between 1905 and 1908. The work duty was light, leaving Barton time to enjoy her home at Glen Echo and a summer mansion she had purchased in Oxford, Massachusetts.

Even in her eighties, Barton rose, made a fire, and prepared breakfast, as she had done for so many years. One reporter arrived to find her fixing part of her sidewalk. When he inquired as to whether it would be better to hire someone else to do this job, she replied that she was grateful to have the energy and strength to perform it at her age.

If there was a down note to Barton's last years, it was the disappearance of friends and family. One of her

Edith Wilson, widow of President Woodrow Wilson (*left*), and Helen Taft, widow of President William Howard Taft (*right*), attended the annual meeting of the national volunteer service committee of the American Red Cross on December 14, 1933, in Washington, D.C. They are shown with the chair of the committee, Mabel T. Boardman (*center*), who had forced Barton to resign the presidency of the American Red Cross years earlier.

beloved nephews Stevie remained and was often with her at the Oxford house in the summer. She also had grand-nephews and grandnieces, but Barton was the last of her own generation. Her brother Stephen had died in 1865, and her beloved brother David had died—possibly of suicide—in 1888. Yet people who came to visit found that she talked at least as much about the future as the past. She was interested in the advent of electricity and the appearance of the automobile, and she thought things looked bright for the twentieth century.

In 1909, Barton traveled alone to Chicago, by train, to take part in a gathering of Union Army veterans. She received the cheers and whistles she had known 50 years earlier, and the event seemed to lighten her spirits. But this was her last major trip, and by 1910, she was confined to home.

Barton's last months and weeks were spent in and out of dreams. There were times when she was astonishingly clear-minded, and when she could remember all sorts of wonderful things from the past. Then there were days and moments when she seemed in a dream state. If age had taken much from her, it also seemed to give her more peace than she had ever previously enjoyed. Like many older people, Barton slowly gave up the burden of responsibility.

Her last days came in April 1912. Her nephew Stevie and Dr. Julian Hubbell were with her in the last moments. She seemed, for a moment, to recover, and then called out, "Let me go, let me go!" She passed away, seconds later, at the age of 90.[1]

REMEMBERING CLARA BARTON

Clara Barton's contributions are memorialized at her last home in Glen Echo, Maryland. The house, once the headquarters for the American Red Cross and a warehouse for emergency supplies, offers guided tours and is open to visitors. Established as the Clara Barton National Historic Site in 1975, Barton's Glen Echo home and the Clara Barton Birthplace Museum in Oxford, Massachusetts, are dedicated to preserving the memory of Barton's accomplishments.

HER LASTING LEGACY

Barton lived a rich, fulfilling life, but there were so many periods of frustration and anxiety that she was less aware than many other people of her own success. Even victories such as establishing the Red Cross (1881) and having it incorporated (1901) were bittersweet, with rivals and foes winning battles against her. Barton suffered from many difficulties in life, a good many of which she caused herself. Though she lived to 90, she never learned to take criticism in a nonjudgmental way. She imagined enemies when they were merely opponents, and there were even times when she unjustly suspected her friends and relatives of disloyalty.

Barton had an amazing ability for friendship and intimacy, but she was too quick to remember any sort of slight or offense to her dignity. Some of her strongest supporters eventually turned away from her, while a handful of others remained loyal to her for as long as she lived. Although plenty of women of her time remained unwed, Barton felt the sting of never having married.

On the other hand, her professional legacy was lasting and secure. At the time of her death, Barton was arguably the most admired of all American women, and she had enjoyed that role for at least a generation. Most Americans knew little of her personal struggles, or the clashes over Red Cross leadership. Instead, they remembered the wonderful tales of Barton at Antietam, in Turkey, and after the Battle of San Juan Hill. Within a decade, her name was in nearly all the textbooks of U.S. history; her life story was a testament to what a determined woman could achieve. She has never been removed from this well-deserved place.

A single book cannot fully summarize a life as rich as Barton's own. Still, historians can pose these questions: Was Barton a feminist? Not in the modern sense of the word. Was she a humanitarian? Beyond any doubt. Did she

Clara Barton, as photographed in 1904, the year she resigned from the American Red Cross. Eighty-two years old at the time of her retirement, she had been the president of the American Red Cross for 22 years.

believe in the ability of men and women to make the world a better place? Absolutely.

And so history is left with a stunningly rich portrait of this shy girl from Massachusetts who became the toast of Civil War veterans, the woman who enjoyed more honors than any woman of her time, the lifelong admirer of men who never married, the advocate for women who never fully got on board with the feminist movement. Clara Barton was, like so many of us, more than the sum of her parts.

CHRONOLOGY

1821	Clarissa Harlow Barton born in Oxford, Massachusetts.
1839	Barton begins teaching school.
1851	Attends Clinton Liberal Institute in New York.
1854	Moves to Washington, D.C.
1854–1857	Barton is employed by the U.S. Patent Office.
1857	Returns to Oxford, Massachusetts.
1860	Returns to Washington, D.C.
1861	Assists soldiers of the 21st Massachusetts and collects medical supplies.
1862	Barton buries her father in Oxford; collects supplies and rushes to battlefields of Cedar Mountain, Chantilly, and Antietam.
1863	Goes to Hilton Head, South Carolina; observes Battle for Fort Wagner.
1864	Returns to Washington, D.C.
1865	Barton's brother and nephew die in the same season. Abraham Lincoln is assassinated in April.
1866–1867	Goes on lecture tour through North and Midwest.
1868	Leaves for Europe for a long rest.
1869	Learns of the International Red Cross.
1870	Volunteers to help with wounded in Franco-Prussian War.
1871	Spends time in war-stricken Paris.

1872   Lives in London before returning to Washington, D.C.

1881   Appeals to President Garfield to sign the Geneva Accords. Garfield is assassinated this year; Barton establishes the American Red Cross and serves as its president.

1882   President Chester A. Arthur signs U.S. agreement to the Geneva Conventions.

1884   Barton assists people in flood-stricken Midwest.

1889   Barton helps flood victims in Johnstown, Pennsylvania.

1893   The Red Cross sends assistance to Russians in time of famine and spends four months helping South Sea Islanders after hurricane.

1896   Travels to Turkey, leading a rescue effort for Armenians.

1898   Travels to Cuba, on the request of President William McKinley; enters Santiago de Cuba aboard *State of Texas*.

1902   Attends seventh conference of International Red Cross.

1904   Resigns as president of the American Red Cross.

1905   Forms the National First Aid Society and serves as its president.

1912   Clara Barton dies on April 12 in Glen Echo, Maryland, and is buried in Oxford, Massachusetts.

NOTES

CHAPTER 1: THE BLOOD OF ANTIETAM

1. Barton, William E., *The Life of Clara Barton, Founder of the American Red Cross*, Boston: Houghton Mifflin, 1922, 1: p. 194–195.
2. Ibid., p. 200
3. Ibid., p. 206.
4. Oates, Stephen B., *A Woman of Valor: Clara Barton and the Civil War*, New York: The Free Press, 1994, p. 86.
5. Pryor, Elizabeth Brown, *Clara Barton: Professional Angel*, Philadelphia: University of Pennsylvania Press, 1987, p. 89.

CHAPTER 2: NOTHING BUT FEAR

1. Barton, Clara, *The Story of My Childhood*, New York: Baker and Taylor, 1907, p. 17.
2. Ibid., p. 23.
3. Ibid., pp. 113–114.

CHAPTER 4: FOLLOW THE CANNON

1. Barton, *The Life of Clara Barton*, p. 110.
2. Pryor, *Clara Barton*, p. 84.
3. Barton, *The Life of Clara Barton*, p. 173.
4. Ibid., p. 81.
5. Ibid., pp. 182–183.

CHAPTER 5: GUNPOWDER BLUE

1. Bowman, John S., ed., *Facts About the American Wars*, New York: H.W. Wilson, 1998, p. 285.
2. Oates, *A Woman of Valor*, p. 108.
3. Barton, *The Life of Clara Barton*, p. 210.

CHAPTER 6: A NEW NATION

1. Pryor, *Clara Barton*, p. 134.

CHAPTER 7: RED ON WHITE

1. Barton, Clara, *The Red Cross: A History of this Remarkable International Movement in the Interest of Humanity*, Washington, D.C.: American National Red Cross, 1898, pp. 57–58.
2. Barton, *The Life of Clara Barton*, p. 87.

CHAPTER 9: WORKING OVERSEAS

1. Pryor, *Clara Barton*, p. 303.
2. Barton, *The Life of Clara Barton*, p. 284.
3. Pryor, *Clara Barton*, p. 309.
4. Ross, Ishbel, *Angel of the Battlefield: The Life of Clara Barton*, New York: Harper & Brothers Publishers, 1956, p. 219.

CHAPTER 10: LAST BATTLES

1. Pryor, *Clara Barton*, p. 372.

BIBLIOGRAPHY

Barton, Clara. *The Red Cross: A History of this Remarkable International Movement in the Interest of Humanity*. Washington, D.C.: American National Red Cross, 1898.

Barton, William E. *The Life of Clara Barton, Founder of the American Red Cross*. 2 vols. Boston: Houghton Mifflin, 1922.

Burton, David H. *Clara Barton: In the Service of Humanity*. Westport, Conn.: Greenwood Press, 1995.

Oates, Stephen B. *A Woman of Valor: Clara Barton and the Civil War*. New York: The Free Press, 1994.

Pryor, Elizabeth Brown. *Clara Barton: Professional Angel*. Philadelphia: University of Pennsylvania Press, 1987.

Young, Charles Sumner. *Clara Barton: A Centenary Tribute*. Boston: The Gorham Press, 1922.

FURTHER RESOURCES

BOOKS

Gilbo, Patrick F. *The American Red Cross: The First Century*. New York: Harper & Row, 1981.

Moorehead, Caroline. *Dunant's Dream: War, Switzerland, and the History of the Red Cross*. New York: Carroll & Graf, 1999.

Turk, Michele. *Blood, Sweat and Tears: An Oral History of the American Red Cross*. Robbinsville, N.J.: E Street Press, 2006.

WEB SITES

American Red Cross
http://www.redcross.org

Clara Barton Homestead
http://www.nps.gov/history/nr/travel/pwwmh/ma41.htm

International Committee of the Red Cross
http://www.icrc.org

PICTURE CREDITS

INDEX

ABOUT THE AUTHOR

SAMUEL WILLARD CROMPTON lives in the Berkshire Hills of Massachusetts, about 60 miles west of Clara Barton's hometown. As a boy, he became interested in the Civil War, both from visiting battlefields and from playing war games at home. He is a major contributor to the American National Biography, published by Oxford University Press, and has written a number of books for Chelsea House. He teaches history at Westfield State College and Holyoke Community College in his native western Massachusetts.